Philosophy in Schools

In 1972, Matthew Lipman founded the Institute of Advancement for Philosophy for Children (IAPC), producing a series of novels and teaching manuals promoting philosophical inquiry at all levels of schooling. The programme consisted of stories about children discussing traditional topics of ethics, values, logic, reality, perception, and politics as they related to their own daily experiences. Philosophy for Children has been adapted beyond the IAPC texts, but the process remains one of an open community of inquiry in which teachers promote respect, conceptual clarity, critical judgement, and active listening without imposing their own ideas.

Philosophy in Schools describes the successes and difficulties in implementing this community of inquiry model. The book covers topics including the formation of non-didactic courses in ethics, the difficulties of fitting a post-compulsory philosophy course into a standard curriculum framework, and the political assumptions of adopting this model in low socioeconomic schools. The contributions also ask deeper questions about how a genuine community of inquiry model is incompatible with conventional models of schooling, with their positioning of the discipline of philosophy in the curriculum. This book was originally published as a special issue of *Educational Philosophy and Theory*.

Felicity Haynes is a retired Education researcher, who formerly taught at The University of Western Australia, Perth, Australia. Her research and teaching focuses on critical thinking, ethics, conceptual change, gender issues, and education. She founded the Association for Philosophy in Schools in Western Australia in 1987, and has been an active member of the Philosophy of Education Society of Australasia.

T0347520

Educational Philosophy and Theory
Series Editor: Peter Roberts
University of Canterbury, New Zealand

This series is devoted to cutting-edge scholarship in educational philosophy and theory. Each book in the series focuses on a key theme or thinker and includes essays from a range of contributors. To be published in the series, a book will normally have first appeared as a special issue of *Educational Philosophy and Theory*, one of the premier philosophy of education journals in the world. This provides an assurance for readers of the quality of the work and enhances the visibility of the book in the international philosophy of education community. Books in this series combine creativity with rigour and insight. The series is intended to demonstrate the value of diverse theoretical perspectives in educational discourse, and contributors are invited to draw on literature, art and film as well as traditional philosophical sources in their work. Questions of educational policy and practice will also be addressed. The books published in this series will provide key reference points for subsequent theoretical work by other scholars, and will play a significant role in advancing philosophy of education as a field of study.

Titles in the series include

Education, Ethics and Existence
Edited by Peter Roberts

Shifting Focus
Strangers and Strangeness
Edited by Peter Roberts

Philosophy in Schools
Edited by Felicity Haynes

Philosophy in Schools

Edited by
Felicity Haynes

Routledge
Taylor & Francis Group

LONDON AND NEW YORK

First published 2016
by Routledge

2 Park Square, Milton Park, Abingdon, Oxfordshire OX14 4RN
711 Third Avenue, New York, NY 10017

Routledge is an imprint of the Taylor & Francis Group, an informa business

First issued in paperback 2017

British Library Cataloguing in Publication Data
A catalogue record for this book is available from the British Library

ISBN 13: 978-1-138-64110-5 (hbk)
ISBN 13: 978-1-138-30973-9 (pbk)

Typeset in Plantin
by RefineCatch Limited, Bungay, Suffolk

Publisher's Note
The publisher accepts responsibility for any inconsistencies that may have
arisen during the conversion of this book from journal articles to book chapters,
namely the possible inclusion of journal terminology.

Disclaimer
Every effort has been made to contact copyright holders for their permission to
reprint material in this book. The publishers would be grateful to hear from any
copyright holder who is not here acknowledged and will undertake to rectify
any errors or omissions in future editions of this book.

Contents

Citation Information

The chapters in this book were originally published in *Educational Philosophy and Theory*, volume 46, issue 11 (October 2014). When citing this material, please use the original page numbering for each article, as follows:

Chapter 6
Philosophy, Art or Pedagogy? How should children experience education?
Christine Doddington
Educational Philosophy and Theory, volume 46, issue 11 (October 2014) pp. 1258–1269

Chapter 7
Kaupapa Māori, Philosophy and Schools
Georgina Stewart
Educational Philosophy and Theory, volume 46, issue 11 (October 2014) pp. 1270–1275

Chapter 8
School and the Limits of Philosophy
Peter Fitzsimons
Educational Philosophy and Theory, volume 46, issue 11 (October 2014) pp. 1276–1289

Chapter 9
Opening Teachers' Minds to Philosophy: The crucial role of teacher education
Sue Knight and Carol Collins
Educational Philosophy and Theory, volume 46, issue 11 (October 2014) pp. 1290–1299

Chapter 10
What is Philosophy for Children? From an educational experiment to experimental education
Nancy Vansieleghem
Educational Philosophy and Theory, volume 46, issue 11 (October 2014) pp. 1300–1310

For any permission-related enquiries please visit:
http://www.tandfonline.com/page/help/permissions

Notes on Contributors

Leon Benade is Senior Lecturer and Director of Research in the School of Education at Auckland University of Technology, New Zealand. He has a career in education that spans 27 years. Recently he has engaged in independent consultancy work with schools. He believes in the power of critical thinking, so he considers philosophy in schools as a serious endeavour.

Philip Cam is Associate Professor in the School of Humanities and Languages at the University of New South Wales, Sydney, Australia. He is an international authority on philosophy in schools, and is the author of many books on philosophy for teachers and students. His most recent book is *Teaching Ethics in Schools* (2012), and he was the author of an ethics pilot in New South Wales public schools, which led to the introduction of ethics as an alternative to special religious education.

Carol Collins researches and teaches within the School of Education at the University of South Australia, Adelaide, Australia. Her research interests include the development of justificatory reasoning skills and embedding philosophy in school curricula across the year levels. She previously served as co-editor of the ERA B-ranked scholarly publication, *Critical & Creative Thinking: The Australasian Journal of Philosophy in Education*.

Christine Doddington is a Senior Lecturer in Education at the University of Cambridge, UK. She directed the primary wing of the Nuffield funded project 'Improving Learning: The Pupil's Agenda', and was director of the Ofsted funded research project, 'Sustaining Pupils' Progress at Year 3'. She is a member of the International Advisory Board of the journal *Education 3–13*, and associate director for *The Cambridge Primary Review*. She is the co-author of *Child-centred Education: Reviving the Creative Tradition* (with Mary Hilton, 2007).

Peter Fitzsimons is an independent researcher and educational management consultant, having managed an Early Childhood Teachers College for four years. He was associate editor of *Educational Philosophy and Theory* for several years, and has presented numerous conference papers for the Philosophy of Education Society of Australasia. His writing explores the relationship between ethics and social policy, and with a recent PhD in Education, he has published two books and a number of international peer-reviewed journal articles. He served as president of the Philosophy of Education Society of Australasia for three years, and was recently appointed a fellow of the Society.

Felicity Haynes is a retired Education researcher, who formerly taught at The University of Western Australia, Perth, Australia. Her research and teaching focuses on critical thinking, ethics, conceptual change, gender issues, and education. She founded the Association for Philosophy in Schools in Western Australia in 1987, and has been an active member of the Philosophy of Education Society of Australasia.

Sue Knight is lead curriculum author for Primary Ethics, the organization responsible for delivering ethics classes as an alternative to scripture in NSW public schools. She previously taught at the University of South Australia, Adelaide, Australia. Her research interests include the development of justificatory reasoning skills and embedding philosophy in school curricula across the year levels.

Tomaž Lašič is a secondary school teacher in humanities, and currently education researcher at Moodle.com. He is interested in how particular (uses of) digital technologies can challenge the unexamined notion of 'good education' and affect the Deleuzian 'becoming' of actors in the educational process.

Stephan Millett is Chair of the Human Research Ethics Committee at Curtin University, Perth, Australia; foundation director of the Curtin Centre for Applied Ethics and Philosophy; and ethics specialist with the Faculty of Health Sciences. He wrote the course of study in philosophy and ethics now being taught under the auspices of the Western Australian Curriculum Council, and has published three textbooks (with Alan Tapper) for the course. Before turning to philosophy, he was a journalist, newspaper editor, and journalism educator.

Janette Poulton is a Lecturer in the School of Education at the Melbourne Institute of Technology, Australia. She has been the education and innovations officer for the Victorian Association for Philosophy in Schools for over a decade, and is currently president of the Australasian Association (FAPSA). Her interest in promoting a thinking culture extends to working with others in a variety of educational contexts: kindergarten, primary, secondary, VCE, gifted, remedial, tertiary, art galleries, the museum, and adult education.

Georgina Stewart (ko Whakarārā te maunga, ko Matauri te moana, ko Ngāti Kura te hapū, ko Ngāpuhi-nui-tonu te iwi) has a Doctorate of Education from Waikato University, Hamilton, New Zealand, which formed the basis of her book *Good Science? The Growing Gap between Power and Education* (2010). She taught science, mathematics, and Te Reo Māori in Māori-medium and English-medium secondary schools in Auckland and Whangarei from 1992 until 2004, and has contributed to national developments in curriculum and assessment since 1993. She works for the University of Auckland's Faculty of Education at the Tai Tokerau campus in Whangarei, New Zealand.

Alan Tapper is a Senior Research Fellow in the John Curtin Institute for Public Policy at Curtin University, Perth, Australia. He has taught philosophy at universities in Perth for 17 years. He wrote *The Family in the Welfare State* (1990). On moral philosophy, he edited a collection of Julius Kovesi's papers, entitled *Values and Evaluations* (1998), and, with Bob Ewin, he republished *Kovesi's Moral Notions* (2004).

Greg Thompson is a Lecturer in the School of Education at Murdoch University, Perth, Australia. Formerly a secondary teacher of history, English, physical education, woodwork, and philosophy and ethics, his research interests lie in using postmodern theories of education to bring about ontological and epistemological change in late-capitalist times. His doctoral thesis looked at the ways in which secondary schools construct powerful visions of what a good student should be and how this manifests itself in the production of student subjectivities. His MEd thesis became a book, *Swings and Round-Abouts: Discourses of Connectedness in Secondary Schools*.

Nancy Vansieleghem is Head of Education at LUCA School of Arts – Campus Sint Lucas Visual Arts, Ghent, Belgium. Her main research interests are in philosophy of dialogue and public space, following Bakhtin. She emphasises the importance of the simple bare life of the living organism as opposed to the normed good life of the polis, and has published several articles exploring alternative forms of educational practices and experiments in terms of actions that seek to address the forces of the market.

Introduction

Generally acknowledged to be the originator of Philosophy for Children (P4C), Matthew Lipman, with Ann Margaret Sharp, founded the Institute of Advancement for Philosophy for Children (IAPC) in New Jersey in 1972. He sought to develop reasoning skills by teaching logic (Lipman, 1988), especially because he disagreed with the then fashionable Piagetian view that preadolescent children were incapable of formal operations, but he sought to teach philosophy indirectly through discussion of dramatic stories about a community of students. *Harry Stottlemeier's discovery* (Lipman, 1974) traces Harry's growing understanding of categorical logic in everyday experiences, but the word 'syllogism' does not appear in the story or the exercises in the accompanying manual. This attempt to make philosophical skills available to young children was said to 'dumb down' the subject, but it has become a part of international education, especially in Brazil. It did not succeed in the USA, partly because, as Knight and Collins (2006) argue, such open critique was not part of the dominant epistemology or prevailing hegemony. In 2010, the IAPC was forced to become financially independent of Montclair State College, and to close its international journal *Thinking*. Three of its most influential members have recently died: Ann Margaret Sharp in July 2010, Matthew Lipman in December 2010 and Gareth Matthews in April 2011.

To some extent the articles in this special issue, drawn from papers delivered at the 2010 40th Annual National Conference of the Philosophy of Education Society of Australasia on the theme of Philosophy in Schools, analyse reasons for the successes and failures of P4C, in particular whether it could succeed in presenting a democratic shift for social change or whether it would have to conform to be a passive subject of an education department regime.

The first general question to be addressed is whether philosophy should be a separate subject in schools, whether taught formally or through P4C. Georgina Stewart, from New Zealand, suggests that it is both ineffective and redundant as a separate subject and the concern to have children think for themselves should be handled in existing subject areas such as social science, philosophy of science and Kura Kaupapa Māori. Chris Doddington suggests that young children could be taught to wonder through philosophy in art and literature subjects.

Stephan Millett and Alan Tapper outline the history of a postcompulsory course in Philosophy and Ethics in Western Australia, warning of the many difficulties of fitting an open-ended subject encouraging students and teachers to respect all views, to a standardized curriculum framework of outcomes and levels required by the Curriculum Council. The course content was traditional, asking the general questions: How do we know? What is real? and How should we live? Keeping an organic and open aspect to make the six units accessible to non-academic students allowed critics to claim that it was not *really* philosophy. However, the textbooks written by Millett and Tapper make explicit reference to philosophers and their ideas, and include exercises in critical thinking and conceptual analysis.

Combining the standard rules of critical thinking with the creativity and openness of making meaning seemed best achieved through an open *community of inquiry*,[1] that shifted the teacher's role from that of the expert didact to a procedural one in which children, given a stimulus material, could set their own agenda of inquiry. The course was entitled Philosophy and Ethics in order to more easily fit the core values of the whole curriculum framework, namely:

- a pursuit of knowledge and a commitment to achievement of potential
- self-acceptance and respect of self
- respect and concern for others and their rights
- social and civic responsibility.

While, in order to meet core curriculum values, ethics became a central part of that philosophy course, religion remained a separate subject in Western Australia for reasons similar to those raised here by Philip Cam. Cam adopts a similar move away from instruction to understanding in arguing that there is an important place in schools for a reflective discussion of ethical values rather than traditional religious instruction. His premise is that both ethics and philosophy cannot simply be taught by learning the facts *or* learning obedience, but that they must accelerate the disposition to give reasons, the autonomy of independent judgement. He believed that the optional religious studies available in New South Wales primary state schools was too prescriptive to be effective. Cam was instrumental in providing philosophy sessions in ethics in schools as an alternative to religious education and free time.

Peter Fitzsimons believes that if philosophy is offered as a standardized school subject, through direct instruction, using analytical tools of critical thinking and the writings of past philosophers, it remains a harmless philosophy, to be distinguished from this more child-centred subject called philosophy which allows independent judgement and encourages a critical capacity. The latter becomes a 'dangerous' philosophy, following Nietzsche, because it liberates the leaders of the future from past politics. However, this dangerous philosophy remains basically inconsistent with the political functions of schooling, as Greg Thompson and Tomaž Lašič suggest, using the metaphor of a smooth space as opposed to nomadic territory in which students in a low socioeconomic school in Western Australia are free to explore Millett's course by authentic inquiry and critique. Despite its popularity and apparent success in achieving its transformative aims, the 'liberating' philosophy course they offered was removed by a principal who had more sedate expectations of subjects in schools, illustrating Fitzsimons' point.

The consequence of teaching philosophy as a harmless subject like this is, to quote Nancy Vansieleghem, that 'thinking for oneself ceases to be the external expression of an inner truth … and becomes a matter of acquired competences, knowledge and skills of self-government and self-awareness'. Several articles in this issue voice a concern that in its tolerance and even celebration of difference, philosophy is basically incompatible with institutionalized schooling. Does the community of inquiry by encouraging independent thinking in students in itself help them to become more philosophical? Cam elsewhere has promoted the idea of a Question Quadrant in which questions of meaning and comprehension can mainly be fitted into an open-ended section using imagination, but those questions to which there is no set answer and which raise deeper issues go into a 'philosophical' quadrant called inquiry.

From Belgium, Vansieleghem suggests that the community of inquiry did offer the opportunity for meaningful experiences and discovery to replace the economic and bureaucratic considerations that drove a school's agenda. Yet Thompson and Lašič criticize community of inquiry for privileging 'those students who come from a background that is immersed in verbal debate and have a firm grasp of English that allows them to structure coherent and rational responses. It assumes that these students will have a tradition in understanding academic arguments and criticism, or an expectation that it can learned quickly', implying that even the community of inquiry has a sociopolitical bias. Thompson and Lašič nevertheless indicate that their rhizomatic philosophy, especially with the help of internet programmes, improved thinking in other subject areas, allowing students to critique their wonder and imagination obtained in literature. The question remains as to whether this is, strictly speaking, *philosophical* thinking.

Vansieleghem suggests that although the commitment to an open community of inquiry was driven by a postmodern desire to disrupt traditional hegemonies, it historically resulted in many teachers moving too far away from Lipman's early emphasis on critical thinking skills. In a typically Lyotardian move, she deconstructs the attempt to construct a self through dialogue and self-'correction' as a grand narrative, and leaves us with subjectivities continuously reconstructing themselves in the face of complex contradictions. The role of philosophy becomes not giving critical thinking skills, but presenting challenging and risky symbolic spaces, contexts or zones. This evolution of philosophy to changing subjectivities may seem far removed from Lipman's project, but is not inconsistent with Dewey's organic evolution of self.

Doddington had suggested that the focus on Deweyan pragmatism and critical thinking had perhaps moved primary classes in particular too far away from the philosophy of wonder, and suggested that discussing storytelling through art and literature is more important at this level than critical thinking skills. Lipman wanted to develop critical thinking skills which attached themselves to children's experiences in the world. He defined critical thinking as thinking that (1) facilitates judgement because it (2) relies on criteria, (3) is self-correcting, and (4) is sensitive to context, and did indeed use dramatic stories to stimulate discussion. Wonder, caring and context were as important to Lipman as the development of reasonableness. But the question remains as to whether literature and the arts can make philosophy redundant.

Fitzsimons pays respect to Maxine Greene, existentialist champion of the arts in schools, to support his requirement of engagement with freedom in philosophy. The challenge for educators is to engage as many as possible in the thought that is freedom, by developing a concern for the critical and the imaginative. Instead of turning to literature and the arts, however, he turns to the idea of valuing care over reason using Nietzsche's hammer as a pivot. This shifts the emphasis away from reasoning skills to ethics.

The Rasch model of traits analysis used by Janette Poulton to construct a middle years curriculum framework of bands and strands, also underpinned the WA curriculum framework of bands and strands that was the foundation of Millett's Philosophy and Ethics course. However, rather than being proscribed by economic accountability, Poulton offers empirical research to justify an alternative curriculum framework to that offered by Millett, based on the empathetic dimension and moving through creative thinking to a critical dimension.[2] Her research showed that a hierarchical frame of critical thinking tools, almost Piagetian, was less appropriate to evaluate progress than the development of strategies of discourse: 'the ability to form a complex point of view, to bear in mind multiple perspectives and theoretical positions, and to evaluate that point of view according to objective criteria', necessary for a community of inquiry. Poulton uses her data to build her framework not around 'the mastery or internalization of standard rules of critical thinking, but (on) a disposition to be fair in considering alternative positions; that is, it is the development of a civil and ethical disposition', vindicating both Cam's and Millett's assumption that building a community of inquiry places ethics at the core, with 'being reasonable' a more significant outcome than thinking logically.[3]

Splitter and Sharp (1995, p. 6) summed up the aims of philosophy for children as reasonableness, adding: 'Reasonableness is primarily a social disposition: the reasonable person respects others and is prepared to take into account their views and their feelings, to the extent of changing her own mind about issues of significance, and consciously allowing her own perspective to be changed by others. She is, in other words, willing to be reasoned with'. As Leon Benade suggests it should be, this makes critical thinking pragmatic and contextual, leaving philosophy in schools open to the possibility of a shift from political control to a genuinely participatory democracy. This is echoed in Fitzsimons' reference to Nietzsche, who names reason as the cause of our falsification of the evidence of the senses.

Benade's analytical comparison of the secondary philosophy programmes in Western Australia and New Zealand highlights the more consistent focus in Western Australia on philosophical skills in a cognitive framework, claiming that the tighter structure allows greater freedom from a conservative political curriculum, an issue denied by Stewart, who says that on the evidence of philosophical aspects in other subject areas in New Zealand schools, teaching philosophical skills does not achieve the democratization claimed by philosophy in schools.

Millett advocates increasing philosophical training in teacher education but Sue Knight and Carol Collins' article claims that both teachers and teacher training institutions do not value a critical or philosophical disposition to enquire. In many respects teacher training remains safe in reinforcing the mood of the political hegemony of the educational institution as a whole.

So should philosophy be a subject in schools? It can easily be if it is limited by the curricular requirements of standardized assessment procedures and knowledge about philosophy and critical thinking skills, but as is shown in this issue the concept of philosophy remains contentious. Philosophy in schools has been variously described in this issue as:

- 'knowledge of philosophy, deductive logic and critical reasoning' (Thompson and Laszic)
- in common with all school subjects, 'a pursuit of knowledge and a commitment to achievement of potential; self-acceptance and respect of self; respect and concern for others and their rights; social and civic responsibility' (Millett and Tapper)
- development of 'the capacity for morally responsible democratic dispositions' through critical thinking (Doddington)
- cultivating a disposition to look for and furnish reasons (Vansieleghem)
- a tool to generate critical, creative and caring thinking (Lipman, cited by Stewart)
- a form of engagement that is characterized by a freedom to wonder and by a lack of thought centred on direct action or necessity, forging both personal and cultural identity (Fitsimons).

This is not a simple continuum from teacher-centred instruction to child-centred imagination. Through the community of inquiry one learns the judgement necessary to adjust critically to the values of others or persuade others to adjust, and that requires the tools of reasonableness. Ironically, Piaget recommends that the only way to rise to a level of formal abstractions is to suffer disequilibrium to one's own schemata, and the community of inquiry offers just that jolt to one's presumptions and opinions. The core family resemblance is represented in the capacity of the community of inquiry to engage the child emotionally as well as intellectually, to link and connect ideas, to challenge them to give and seek reasons for different points of view, to demand conceptual clarity and to create a disposition to understand rather than dismiss opposing views, all of which should lead to an awareness of each child's place in a fluid and growing community where difference is celebrated.

This is the pragmatism that Lipman borrowed from Dewey, shifting the emphasis from Truth to truths, from Philosophy to philosophies. The skills of critical thinking are important only insofar as they assist communication and exchange of values and meaning, insofar, as Lipman reminds us, as they contribute to reasonableness.

For the time being, let us remain at the level of a Deweyan pragmatism and place our faith in the sharing of dialogue through a community of open inquiry (Pardales & Girod, 2006), with perhaps supplementary lessons in critical thinking and the writings of earlier philosophers. The community of inquiry has a structure which evokes the spirit of cooperation, care, trust, safety, and a sense of common purpose and inquiry, which, in turn, evokes a form of self-correcting practice driven by the need to transform that which is intriguing, problematic, confused, ambiguous or fragmentary into some kind of unifying whole which is satisfying to those involved (Lipman, 1993a, 1993b, 2003). More importantly, it engages the whole mind including the imagination, and social awareness (hooks, 2010, p. 43).

That seems to be an important reason for making philosophy in schools not only a separate subject at all levels of schooling, but in its transformatory capacity informing all other subject areas.

Notes

1. It is referred to variously in different articles in this issue as community of inquiry (Coi), Community of Philosophical Inquiry (COPI) and Community of Philosophical Enquiry (CoPE). Lipman described a **community of inquiry** as the social and educational context that leads to 'questioning, reasoning, connecting, deliberating, challenging, and developing problem-solving techniques'. Drawn from C. S. Pierce, it was a holistic and organic understanding of a community of students and teachers engaged in authentic inquiry. The pedagogical process is summarized on p. 64 of this issue.
2. She is referring to the middle years of schooling, while Millett was offering a course leading to an external matriculation examination.
3. A full discussion of the relationship of a community of inquiry to ethics and the ideal of a participatory democracy is offered by Gilbert Burgh (Burgh, Field, & Freakley 2006).

References

Burgh, G., Field, T., & Freakley, M. (2006). *Ethics and the community of inquiry: Education for deliberative democracy*. South Melbourne: Thomson/Social Science Press.

hooks, bell (2010). *Teaching critical thinking: Practical wisdom*. New York: Routledge.

Knight, S., & Collins, C. (2006). Cultivating reason-giving: The primary purpose of education? *International Journal of the Humanities, 3*, 187–194.

Lipman, M. (1974). *Harry Stottlemeier's discovery*. New Jersey: Institute for the Advancement of Philosophy for Children.

Lipman, M. (1988). *Philosophy goes to school*. Philadelphia, PA: Temple University Press.

Pardales, M., & Girod, M. (2006). Community of inquiry: Its past and present future. *Educational Philosophy and Theory, 38*, 299–309.

Splitter, L., & Sharp, A. M. (1995). *Teaching for better thinking: The classroom community of inquiry*. Hawthorn, Vic.: Australian Council for Educational Research.

Felicity Haynes
The University of Western Australia

Philosophy for Children, Values Education and the Inquiring Society

PHILIP CAM

School of Humanities, University of New South Wales

Abstract

How can school education best bring about moral improvement? Socrates believed that the unexamined life was not worth living and that the philosophical examination of life required a collaborative inquiry. Today, our society relegates responsibility for values to the personal sphere rather than the social one. I will argue that, overall, we need to give more emphasis to collaboration and inquiry rather than pitting students against each other and focusing too much attention on 'teaching that' instead of 'teaching how'. I will argue that we need to include philosophy in the curriculum throughout the school years, and teach it through a collaborative inquiry which enables children to participate in an open society subject to reason. Such collaborative inquiry integrates personal responsibility with social values more effectively than sectarian and didactic religious education.

Introduction[1]

As Socrates would have it, the philosophical examination of life is a collaborative inquiry. The social nature of the enterprise goes with its spirit of inquiry to form his bifocal vision of the examined life. These days, insofar as our society teaches us to think about values, it tends to inculcate a private rather than a public conception of them. This makes reflection a personal and inward journey rather than a social and collaborative one, and a person's values a matter of parental guidance in childhood and individual decision in maturity. The relegation of responsibility for values to the personal sphere also militates against societal self-examination.

On the other hand, the traditional pontifical alternative is equally presumptive and debilitating in ignoring the possibility of personal judgement. How can education steer a course between the tyranny of unquestionable moral codes and the bankruptcy of individualistic moral relativism? It remains to be seen whether there is a way in which

7

education could teach children to engage productively across their differences rather than responding to difference with suspicion or prejudice.

Gilbert Ryle (in Cahn, 1970) made a clear distinction between 'teaching how' and 'teaching that', arguing from a behaviourist perspective that teaching how had a much more lasting impact than simply teaching the facts. However, too much emphasis on 'teaching how' can result in conditioning, training, teaching to conform to habit, teaching obedience with the threat of hellfire if the rules are broken. There is a third way, the way of philosophy espoused by Matthew Lipman (2002) in his Philosophy for Children, which involves giving more emphasis to collaboration and inquiry rather than pitting students against each other and focusing too much attention on 'teaching that' instead of 'teaching how'. Philosophy as it is traditionally taught may well involve teaching how to follow the rules of formal logic correctly, or learning facts about the life and death of Socrates, but it also requires a capacity for critical reflection, consideration of alternative possibilities, and a genuine concern for truth and clarity.

I argue that we need to include philosophy in the curriculum throughout the school years, but it needs to be a philosophy taught in the spirit of Socrates which balances individual and social values. Religious instruction tends to inculcate values through adult imposition and denies space to critical judgement.

Ryle's distinction between 'learning that' and 'learning how' implied that these were discrete and exclusive ways of learning. However, learning how to do things is more than a matter of memorizing facts or following procedural instructions. Being able to cook is more than being able to follow a recipe book. Again, while some instruction is useful in learning to ride a bike, it is mostly a matter of trying to ride, and then, under guidance, trying again. It is a case of learning by doing, and doing it under different circumstances, in order to apply it in different circumstances. This is working out for oneself how to exercise individual judgement, rather than first learning a set of instructions and then carrying them out (Ryle, in Cahn, 1970, pp. 413–424). Whatever the rules are, they are heuristic and strategic, depending on different contexts, rather than algorithmic and learnable by rote.

'Learning how' can be important in many areas of the curriculum where training in skills is an important feature, especially in physical education and the arts, However, learning the art of inquiry requires a slightly different type of 'learning how' from training, rehearsal, repetition. A curriculum that is based on inquiry is one that is centred on thinking. There is a world of difference in the outcome to be expected from an education that treats knowledge as material with which to think and one that emphasizes memorization of knowledge. It is the difference between an inquiring society and one in which those few who have developed an inquiring mind have done so in spite of their education rather than because of it (Dewey, 1916/1966, chap. 12; Lipman, 2002). The concept of a community of inquiry owes much to Dewey who, in *Democracy and education* (1916/1966), described the healthy relation between an individual and his or her environment as functional. Dewey insisted that because the relationship between the individual and his or her environment must be based on mutual adjustment, fitting into society might well involve radically changing it.

Dewey believed in the importance of preparing students for democratic citizen-ship. He stressed that consciously guided education aimed at developing the 'mental equipment' and moral character of students was essential to the development of civic character. Is this not what religious instruction tries to do? The relationship between the individual and society was far more important for Dewey than the child's relation-ship with an abstract God. It was organic and continually evolving in mutual adapta-tion. It differs from religious instruction in that its aim is to develop a model of free inquiry, which requires tolerance of alternative viewpoints, and free communication. He also believed that children's capacity for the exercise of deliberative, practical rea-son in moral situations could be cultivated not by ready-made knowledge but by 'a mode of associated living' characteristic of democracy. Lipman (1988) was to elaborate on this idea of schools as a model of a participatory democracy and his classroom community of inquiry provided close analogies with the democratic school, a microcosm of the wider society.

Thinking Together

When we move away from the traditional classroom to the inquiring one and the tea-cher becomes less occupied with conveying information—with teaching 'that'— it becomes educationally desirable for students to engage with one another. When human conduct stimulates moral inquiry it is usually because that conduct is contro-versial, which is to say that there are different points of view as to how it should be judged. If you and I have different opinions in regard to someone's character or con-duct, then we are both in need of justification and our views are subject to each other's objections. When we make a proposal to solve a practical problem of any com-plexity, we rely upon others who are reasonably well placed for constructive criticism or a better suggestion.

If we want students to grow out of the habit of going with their own first thoughts, to become used to considering a range of possibilities, and to be on the lookout for better alternatives, then we could not do better than to have them learn by exploring issues, problems and ideas together. If we want them to become used to giving rea-sons for what they think, to expect the same of others, and to make productive use of criticism, then we could not go past giving them plenty of practice with their peers. And if we want them to grow up so that they consider other people's points of view, and not to be so closed minded as to think that those who disagree with them must be either ignorant or vicious, then the combination of intellectual and social engage-ment to be found in collaborative inquiry is just the thing. These are all good reasons for having our students learn to inquire together.

Philosophy for Children

More than any other discipline, philosophy is an inquiry into fundamental human prob-lems and issues, where all the general conceptions that animate society come under scru-tiny. Philosophy as a formal discipline played an important part in its place as a matriculation subject in some Australian states, because there were rigorous rules by which its standards could be maintained. This would involve, say, **learning that** *ignoratio* *elenchi* was an informal fallacy, or that *modus tollens* is an illegitimate move in deductive logic, or **learning how** to mount a reasoned argument in defence of a position.

When, however, we are talking abut philosophy for children, its subject matter needs to be adapted to the interests and experience of students of various ages and its tools and procedures adjusted to their stage of development. There are models to work from, particularly the series of novels and manuals from Matthew Lipman, and in recent years we have begun to find our way forward.[2] If part of the difficulty is also that some philosophers think of philosophy as being above all that, it is salutary to remember that other disciplines have long since discovered how to recast themselves in educational form.

Just as mathematics was forced to become more practical and relevant to the growing range of children who were staying on at school through the New Maths, so philosophy has been forced to become more real and relevant to children. The move towards an integrated curriculum away from discrete learning areas also required philosophy to make the connections across and through disciplines, raising the larger questions of epistemology, ontology, aesthetics and, for the purpose of this article, the important area of axiology or values. For philosophy to have a formative influence, and thereby to significantly affect both the way people think and the character of their concerns, it needs to be part of the regular fare throughout the school years. Only by this means can it effectively supply its nutrients to the developing roots of thought or knowing that and action or knowing how.

We need to counter the view that philosophy is an advanced discipline, suitable only for the academically gifted and intellectually mature. Jerome Bruner made famous the startling claim that 'the foundations of any subject may be taught to anybody at any age in some form' (1960, p. 12), and he suggested that the prevailing view of certain disciplines being too difficult for younger students results in our missing important educational opportunities. Bruner called this structure a *spiral curriculum*: one that begins with the child's intuitive understanding of the fundamentals, and then returns to the same basic concepts, themes, issues and problems at increasingly elaborate and more abstract or formal levels over the years. A spiral curriculum is vital for developing the kind of deep understanding that belongs to philosophy and the humanities.

What else is to be gained from building philosophy into the curriculum throughout the school years? It seems to me that an education in philosophical inquiry will assist students to achieve a rich understanding of a wide array of issues and ideas that inform life and society through an increasingly deep inquiry into them. It will help students to think more carefully about issues and problems that do not have a unique solution or a settled decision procedure, but where judgements and decisions can be better or worse in all kinds of ways. Since most of the problems that we face in life and in our society are of that character, the general-purpose tools that students acquire through philosophy will ensure that they are better prepared to face those problems. If philosophy is carried out in the collaborative style envisaged above, then its recipients will also be more likely to tackle such problems collaboratively, and thereby to be more constructive and accommodating with one another. Let me spell all this out a little under the headings of 'thinking', 'understanding' and 'community'.

Thinking

Philosophy is a discipline with a particular focus on thinking. It involves thinkers in the cognitive surveillance of their own thought. It is a reflective practice, in the sense that it involves not only careful thinking about some subject matter, but thinking about that thinking, in an effort to guide and improve it. Since philosophical thinking tends to keep one eye on the thinking process, philosophy can supply the tools that assist the thinker in such tasks as asking probing questions, making needful distinctions, constructing fruitful connections, reasoning about complex problems, evaluating propositions, elaborating concepts, and honing the criteria that are used to make judgements and decisions. Dewey's (2010) five-step model of identifying the problem and placing it in context, making creative and testable hypotheses that move towards a possible solution, analysing the hypotheses in terms of past experience, considering alternative hypotheses that may be more suitable, and checking possible solutions against actual experiences was picked up as a model of individual thinking, especially in science and design work. But in a community of inquiry each of these steps is done from the multiple perspectives of the group at any age, allowing not only the falsifiability of any conservative position to truth but also their complete contingency.

The skills, abilities and habits of thinking—acquiring the habit of reflecting carefully upon your own thoughts, as well as what others think; developing the ability to imagine and evaluate new possibilities; developing the habit of changing your mind on the basis of good reasons; and acquiring skill in the establishment and use of appropriate criteria to form sound judgements—provide the methodology of Lipman's community of inquiry.

Understanding

Philosophy deals with ethical questions about how we should behave, social questions about the good community, epistemological questions about the justification of people's opinions, metaphysical questions about our spiritual lives, or logical questions about what we may reasonably infer, and is therefore a rich source of our cultural heritage and of contemporary thought and debate. In terms of both its history and ways of thinking, philosophy also helps to deepen our understanding of the big ideas and key concepts that have helped to shape civilization and continue to inform the way we live. Our conceptions of what makes something right or wrong, of justice, freedom and responsibility, of our personal, cultural and national identity, of sources of knowledge, of the nature of truth, beauty and goodness, are all central to what we value and how we conduct our affairs. Since such concepts so deeply inform life and society, it is important for students to develop their understanding of them. While we may attempt to deal with these matters elsewhere in the curriculum, philosophical inquiry gives students the tools that they need in order to explore these ideas in depth.

Community

With regard to cooperative thinking and the importance of community, I would stress the virtues of dialogue. As we work to resolve differences in our understandings, or to subject our reasons to each other's judgement, or try to follow an argument where it leads, we are like detectives whose clues are the experience, inferences, judgements and other intellectual considerations that each thinker brings into the dialogue with others. On this view, philosophical inquiry provides a model of the inquiring community: one that is engaged in thoughtful deliberation and decision making, is driven by a desire to make advance through cooperation and dialogue, and values the kinds of regard and reciprocity that grow under its influence. Just because it has these characteristics, philosophical inquiry can provide a training-ground for people who are being brought up to live together in such a community. Dewey's five steps require the philosophical disposition to give reasons when that is appropriate; and, generally, to cooperate with others and respect different points of view.

Values Education

The vital significance of educating for judgement in regard to values is nowhere more clearly recognized than in the writings of John Dewey: 'The formation of a cultivated and effectively operative good judgment or taste with respect to what is aesthetically admirable, intellectually acceptable and morally approvable is the supreme task set to human beings by the incidents of experience' (Dewey, 1929/1980, p. 262). This makes the cultivation of judgement the ultimate educational task and the development of good judgement central to values education in particular. Values education therefore cannot be simply a matter of instructing students as to what they should value—just so much 'teaching that'—as if students did not need to inquire into values or learn to exercise their judgement. In any case, it is an intellectual mistake to think that values constitute a subject matter to be learned by heart. They are not that kind of thing. Values are embodied in commitments and actions and not merely in propositions that are verbally affirmed.

Nor can values education be reduced to an effort to directly mould the character of students so that they will make the right moral choices—as if in all the contingencies of life there was never really any doubt about what one ought to do, and having the right kind of character would ensure that one did it. Being what is conventionally called 'of good character' will not prevent you from acting out of ignorance, from being blind to the limitations of your own perspective, from being overly sure that you have right on your side, or even from committing atrocities with a good conscience in the name of such things as nation or faith. History is littered with barbarities committed by men reputedly of good character who acted out of self-righteous and bigoted certainty. Far from being on solid moral ground, the ancient tradition that places emphasis upon being made of the right stuff has encouraged moral blindness towards those of different ethnicity, religion, politics, and the like.

Whatever else we do by way of values education, we must make strenuous efforts to cultivate good judgement. When it comes to deciding what to do in a morally troubling situation, good judgement involves distinguishing more from less acceptable decisions and conduct. Such discernment needs to be made by comparing our options in the circumstances in which they occur. Any such comparison requires us to ensure that, insofar as possible, we have hold of all the relevant facts. It involves us doing our best to make sure that we have not overlooked any reasonable course of action. It requires us to think about the consequences of making one decision, or taking one course of action, by comparison with another, and to be mindful of the criteria against which we evaluate them. It requires us to monitor the consequences of our actions in order to adjust our subsequent thinking to actuality. In short, good moral judgement requires us to follow the ways of inquiry. Dewey (1920/1957, pp. 163–164) says:

> A moral situation is one in which judgment and choice are required ante-cedently to overt action. The practical meaning of the situation—that is to say the action needed to satisfy it—is not self-evident. It has to be searched for. There are conflicting desires and alternative apparent goods. What is needed is to find the right course of action, the right good. Hence, inquiry is exacted: observation of the detailed make-up of the situation; analysis into its diverse factors; clarification of what is obscure; discounting of the more insistent and vivid traits; tracing of the consequences of the various modes of action that suggest themselves; regarding the decision reached as hypo-thetical and tentative until the anticipated or supposed consequences which led to its adoption have been squared with the actual consequences.

The lack of integration of our advanced empirical and scientific knowledge with the remnants of value systems of much earlier times is already a problem of consider-able proportions. We should not be adding to this burden when we teach science and technology, or history, or about society and the environment. Instead, we need to introduce our students to ways of thinking that develop their values in conjunction with their other understandings.

This approach to values education fits with the emphasis to be placed upon collab-orative inquiry for several reasons. First, the idea that values are to be cultivated by student reflection rather than impressed upon the student from without by moral authority does not imply that the pursuit of values is a purely personal affair. That would be a pendulum swing to individualistic relativism. Collaborative inquiry sup-plies a middle road—a way forward between an unquestioningly traditional attitude towards values and an individualism that makes each person their own moral author-ity. The development of good judgement through collaborative inquiry is the path towards a truly social intelligence. Secondly, values inquiry depends upon different points of view. If something is uncontroversial and everyone is of the same opinion, then there is no motivation for inquiry. Inquiry arises in situations where something is uncertain, puzzling, contentious or in some way problematic. The collaborative inquiry is organic, synergistic and evolving, a kind of moral practice based on a principle of democracy. Consider such elementary aspects of philosophical practice as: learning to hear someone out when you disagree with what they are saying; learning to explore the source of your disagreement rather than engaging in personal attacks; developing the habit of giving reasons for what you say and expecting the same of others; being disposed to take other people's interests and concerns into account; and generally becoming more communicative and inclusive.

To see values education as continuous with all of our other efforts to educate our young in the ways of inquiry is to place it firmly in the tradition of reflective education rather than traditional religious instruction. Religious instruction cannot take on the burden of a systematic exploration of the ethical issues involved in the various areas of the curriculum as they are presented throughout the rest of the week. If we are to cultivate good moral judgement we need to make it integral to the material that we teach and not something we attempt to establish in such a disconnected fashion. From a pedagogical perspective, while it would be possible for religious instructors to introduce students to values inquiry, they are under no obligation to do so and many of them come from traditions that are likely to use the occasion to moralize and engage in indoctrination instead. This is not to say that religious education is incompatible with values inquiry. It is rather to acknowledge the need for change. Much of traditional religious instruction is antithetical to the educational requirements of an inquiring society; and if we are to develop such a society, such an outdated approach should not retain its foothold in our schools.

This still leaves it open as to whether the school takes a philosophical approach to values education, or insists upon indoctrination rather than education. We should not think of philosophy and religion as representing two incompatible options when it comes to values education. They are representative, however, of a deeper choice that must be made in relation to values education, the choice between appeal to reason and dogmatism as central to the way we teach.

Notes

1. *Editor's Note*: This article has been substantially edited and modified since it was delivered as a keynote address in December 2010. The context in which it was written reflects an ongoing tension between the didactic teaching of ethics through religious education and a more organic process of teaching ethics by modelling it and discussing it in philosophical discussion. In New South Wales (NSW) religious education was not compulsory, but Education Department policy forbade schools from offering alternative lessons to students who chose not to take part in scripture. The NSW government tasked St James Ethics Centre, under the guidance of Professor Cam, to develop and deliver ethics education classes in urban, regional and rural primary schools as an alternative to religious education. St James Ethics Centre promptly established Primary Ethics Limited, an independent not-for-profit organization, to develop an engaging, age-appropriate, interconnected curriculum that spans the primary years from Kindergarten to Year 6 and to then deliver ethics education free of charge via a network of specially trained and accredited volunteers. Despite protests from Church leaders in NSW that they should have sole responsibility for values education, on 1 December 2010 Parliament amended the NSW Education Act to give students who do not attend special religious education/scripture classes in NSW public schools the legal right to attend philosophical ethics classes as an alternative to supervised 'private study'. Because of the popularity of secular ethics classes, pressure from Church leaders and a change to a conservative state government, it was legislated in 2012 that parents should be told of the availability of ethics classes in their school only after they have opted out of special religious education or scripture.
2. Since the early 1990s Lipman's followers have extended his work and this general approach is now represented in schools in many countries around the world. For a selection of Australasian resources see http://www.fapsa.org.au/resources/catalogue

References

Bruner, J. S. (1960). *The process of education*. Cambridge, MA: Harvard University Press.

Cahn, S. E. (Ed.). *The philosophical foundations of education*. New York: Harper & Row.

Dewey, J. (1910). *How we think*. Chicago, IL: D. C. Heath & Co.

Dewey, J. (1957). *Reconstruction in philosophy* (enlarged ed.). Boston, MA: Beacon Press. (Original work published 1920).

Dewey, J. (1966). *Democracy and education*. London: Collier Macmillan. (Original work published 1916).

Dewey, J. (1980). *The quest for certainty*. New York: Perigee Books. (Original work published 1929).

Lipman, M. (1988). *Philosophy goes to school*. Philadelphia, PA: Temple University Press.

Lipman, M. (2002). *Thinking in education* (2nd ed.). New York: Cambridge University Press.

Ryle, G. (1970). Teaching and training. In S.M. Cahn (Ed.), *The philosophical foundations of education* (pp. 413–424). New York: Harper & Row.

Philosophy and Ethics in Western Australian Secondary Schools

STEPHAN MILLETT & ALAN TAPPER

Centre for Applied Ethics and Philosophy, Curtin University

Abstract

The introduction of Philosophy and Ethics to the Western Australian Certificate of Education courses in 2008 brought philosophy into the Western Australian secondary school curriculum for the first time. How philosophy came to be included is part of a larger story about the commitment and perseverance of a relatively small number of Australian educators and their belief in the value of introducing philosophical communities of inquiry into school classrooms through a revised pedagogy which could sit comfortably with an outcomes-based education system.

A Brief History

Philosophy is now included as one of 50 or so subject choices available to Western Australian students entering the final two years of high school. The course, part of the Western Australian Certificate of Education (WACE), enrolled its first students in 2008 and the first group of students sat the final year exams in 2009.

This article concerns the story of how this philosophy course came into being in Western Australian schools. But this is not a purely parochial story, as how Philosophy became part of the WACE, and how it came to have a particular pedagogical approach built in to the curriculum, is a chapter in an international story in which Australia and Australians have played a key role, in particular a group of people who advocate a particular pedagogy to help children *do* philosophy.

Advocacy for philosophy in schools in Australia goes back to about 1984, and begins with Laurance Splitter in Sydney. Splitter had been introduced to Philosophy for Children (P4C) by Matthew Lipman and Ann Sharp at Montclair State University in New Jersey. He then brought Lipman and Sharp to the University of Wollongong in July 1985 to run the first 'Level 2' workshop in Australia. A Level 2 workshop is an intensive week-long course for teachers and philosophers at which participants learn the effective teaching method pioneered by Lipman—a method grounded in Deweyan pragmatism and Vygotskyan psychology. Following the Wollongong workshop, Splitter and others set up the Australian Institute of Philosophy for Children (AIPC). This was a legally constituted national body which initially sold the Lipman texts (e.g. *Harry Stottlemeier's discovery*, Lipman, 1974) before handing that role over to Australian Council for Education Research, and was the forerunner for the current Federation of Australasian Philosophy in Schools Associations (FAPSA).

In 1988 Splitter moved to the Australian Council for Education Research (ACER) in Melbourne and—thanks to the foresight and generosity of then ACER director Barry McGaw—set up a centre for philosophy for children. It is interesting to note McGaw's support of philosophy, which continues today in his role as Chair of the Board of the Australian Curriculum, Assessment and Reporting Authority, as the school-based movement and the Australasian Association of Philosophy combine to lobby for the inclusion of philosophy in the national curriculum. Almost all of the systems have now included philosophy as a secondary school subject. Queensland's programme was first, although it is more specialized than courses in other states; Victoria followed in 2001, South Australia in 2003, Tasmania in 2006 and Western Australia in 2008.[1]

Western Australia

The creation of the Western Australian Philosophy course was set against the background of the formation of the Western Australian Curriculum Council in 1997 and the development of the Curriculum Framework in 1998. The Council and the Framework brought dramatic changes to all schools in WA. The origin of these changes goes back to 1995 and the Review of School Curriculum Development Procedures and Processes in Western Australia, which identified a number of priorities, including the need for:

- a common curriculum direction that enabled curricula to be adapted to the advantage of students
- a seamless curriculum among the different levels of schooling
- greater involvement by non-government schools and the community in state-wide curriculum development processes.

The Curriculum Council was charged with developing a Curriculum Framework, a structure providing a mandatory common and seamless curriculum direction across all levels and all Western Australian schools.

Based on the comparative analysis of courses and the widespread support for the core shared values, Philosophy and Ethics was included as one of the possible courses in the Position Paper. However, a Religion course was not included and it became evident quite early in the next phase of the consultation process that while there was support for a Philosophy and Ethics course there was also a strong lobby for a Religion course. A focus group with a broad spectrum of views across religion and ethics debated the issues and it was clear that a Religion and Life course would be needed. Stephan Millett's memory of that focus group session is of a religious lobby asserting that a Religion course was all that was needed as it could deal adequately with philo-sophical issues. Both courses were subsequently endorsed by the Council and both courses were included in *Our youth, our future*, the Council's review of post-compul-sory education (Western Australia Curriculum Council, 2002).

The Curriculum Council became the overseeing body for the school system state-wide and it became mandatory for all schools, public and private, to adopt the policies developed by the Council. The Council's primary document was the Curriculum Framework, which introduced an 'outcomes-based' philosophy for schooling K-10, and embedded the 'core shared values' into the curriculum. The core shared values were themselves an 'ethics framework' for schooling, and were perhaps the first attempt in Australia to be explicit about values in a largely secular education system.

These core shared values were under four headings:

(1) A pursuit of knowledge and a commitment to achievement of potential
(2) Self-acceptance and respect of self
(3) Respect and concern for others and their rights
(4) Social and civic responsibility.

Under each of these headings was a set of more fine-grained descriptors, such as respecting individual differences, compassion and care; participation and citizenship.

Those educators familiar with P4C could see immediately that in taking part in a philosophical community of inquiry children would demonstrate each of the core shared values, so from the beginnings of the work on the new senior school course in Philosophy it was clear that it was compatible with this core component of the newly mandated framework.

However, after some years of an outcomes-based curriculum and new reporting processes related to it in the primary and middle school years, the Curriculum Council began detailed planning for a new upper school curriculum to replace the existing curriculum. All of the new subjects would be available to all students, whether they were applying for a Tertiary Entrance Ranking (TER) score, for entrance to technical and further education or other further education opportunities. Each new course was to have a syllabus comprising outcomes, essential content and standards.

However, when the 'outcomes' reform process came to be implemented in the upper secondary level, a furore broke out that was to be heard across the country. Four things happened at the same time.

- First, the course offerings for upper secondary were cut from 150 to 52 courses.
- Secondly, a number of new courses were included in the offerings, one of which was Philosophy and Ethics.
- Thirdly, compulsory education was extended to age 17 for the first time, and the newly designed courses had to be accessible to all students, not just those seeking university entrance.

- Fourthly, in the writing or rewriting of the 52 courses, an outcomes approach that had been accepted at lower levels was introduced at the top level.

It was this last change that was fiercely resisted by a section of the senior secondary teachers, perhaps mainly because they had to engage with outcomes in an exam environment, whereas previously, in lower school, teachers could to some degree ignore outcomes or pay lip service to them.

This controversy ran from 2004 until 2009, fuelled by local media with an interest in sensationalized reporting.

Thus, the new Philosophy and Ethics course was born in a time of some turmoil. Stephan Millett was awarded the tender to be the writer for the course. This involved working with a reference group with members from the universities and all sectors of secondary education. Fitting a philosophy course into a bed which was not a natural fit proved demanding. Forcing the course into a predetermined framework was not a problem unique to philosophy, but the goodwill and shared purpose of the reference group helped us to cut and stretch what we felt to be important to fit a mould that also served the more than 50 other courses. The writing of the Philosophy and Ethics course was largely completed in 2005.[2] The course was trialled with action research in 2006, professional development followed from 2007, and the course itself was introduced formally in 2008. It was one of the few courses that kept to the timetable set out for it. In part that smooth introduction is explained by the strong representation on the reference group by members of the Association for Philosophy in Schools (APIS WA), who have been part of the Australian P4C movement and who have a shared understanding of the nature of the subject and of how it may be taught successfully to students with a range of intellectual abilities and cognitive maturity.

Designing the Course

The Philosophy and Ethics course was a completely new curriculum area for Western Australia. It, along with every other course, had to refer specifically to both what were called overarching outcomes and learning area outcomes which together made up the mandatory element of the Framework.[3] The 52 new courses were introduced in three waves. Philosophy and Ethics was part of the second wave and synthesized outcomes from the learning areas of English, Arts, Science, Society and Environment, Media, and Technology and Enterprise. The course was intended to meet the needs of students: who wished to pursue the study of Philosophy and Ethics at tertiary level; who would continue studies in the vocational area; who intended to go straight into the workplace; and those who wished to develop skills for their own development and enjoyment.

In the design of the course, four features are noteworthy.

- The first is that from the outset philosophy was seen as quite distinct from religion.

- The second feature is signalled by its unusual title: Philosophy and Ethics. A number of people pointed out that since ethics is a branch of philosophy, it makes no sense to have it in the title. An explanation of the title can be found in the official Rationale. The title 'Philosophy and Ethics' gives ethics a prominent status, signifying that it has particular importance in this course. This status recognizes that every member of a society faces ethical issues. A philosophical approach helps people to reflect on, and better understand, difficult ethical issues.
- The third feature is that this course had to follow an 'outcomes-based' approach which meant it could not be designed simply as a body of content. It had to have three or four overarching outcomes.
- The fourth feature is that the reference group included people familiar with the techniques and philosophy underpinning P4C. In 1999, Stephan Millett became President of the WA Association for Philosophy in Schools and the association began running workshops for teachers on a regular basis, prompted initially by a group from the district high school in the small south-west town of Pemberton who had visited Buranda primary school in Brisbane.

Through subtle pressure from Felicity Haynes and Stephan Millett the reference group came to understand and then to embrace the Lipman method, the community of inquiry pedagogy, and the various modifications that have been made as P4C was 'Australianized'. This meant that we had a cohesive outlook and a shared understanding of how the course might best be taught. At no stage was there conflict about what we were trying to do and the Curriculum Council gave us full scope to follow our own professional inclinations.

Bases of Pedagogy

The pedagogy is informed by the democratic principles and philosophical pragmatism of John Dewey (1916/1966, 1910/1933, 1920/1957) and the psychology of learning of Lev Vygotsky (1978) in which ways of thinking experienced at the interpersonal level—in listening to the way others think—are internalized to become a model for *intra*personal thinking. That is, each participant learns from dialogic interaction ways of developing effective self-talk, especially when they come to clarifying concepts and resolving problems. This tool, the philosophical community of inquiry, is deceptively simple but is very powerful, and routinely gives the teacher beautiful insights into the rich thinking that children are capable of when they talk and listen to each other in pursuit of conceptual clarity. The course Rationale, when it was finally approved, placed community of inquiry front and centre.

Through essential content, prescribed outcomes and partially prescribed pedagogy a course with six units was devised with the aim of developing in students thinking and analytical skills and moral discernment that may be applied to a range of practical situations in their personal, interpersonal and working lives.

Essential Content

The essential content of the course followed traditional lines, dividing into Metaphysics, Epistemology and Ethics, although these were expressed more colloquially in question form as:

- How do we know?
- What is real?
- How should we live?

These headings were elaborated in considerable detail. Content under 'How do we know?' was divided into: critical reasoning; methods of inquiry; imagination and interpretation; and analysing, clarifying and evaluating concepts. 'What is real?' comprised: scientific worldview; conceptions of ultimate reality; and persons. Content in 'How should we live?' was divided into: Self and others; communities and cultures; and governance. Some of these subdivisions were required by the Curriculum Framework.

Outcomes

Outcomes under the Curriculum Framework are 'statements of what students should know, understand, value and be able to do as a result of the syllabus content taught'. The difficult task of designing suitable outcomes was resolved by settling on four outcomes, as follows:

- *Outcome 1: Philosophical and ethical inquiry*. Here students use investigative methods familiar to philosophers to think and argue philosophically. They participate in open philosophical communities of inquiry; explore philosophical and ethical concepts, ideas and ideals; and use critical reasoning methods to recognize, analyse, evaluate and develop arguments.
- *Outcome 2: Philosophical and ethical perspectives*. Students understand that there are philosophical and ethical approaches to making meaning.
- *Outcome 3: Philosophy and ethics in human affairs*. Students understand that philosophical and ethical thinking has a role in human affairs. In achieving this outcome, students understand that there are philosophical traditions; understand that there are different world views; and understand the influence of philosophical ideas on contemporary culture.
- *Outcome 4: Applying and relating philosophical and ethical understandings*. Students reflect on, evaluate and respond to a range of human issues by selecting from a repertoire of philosophical and ethical strategies.

An outcomes approach actually suits philosophy well, as philosophy can readily be thought of not so much as subject matter to be learned but as a set of skills to be acquired by practice. To quote the Rationale again:

> Philosophy and Ethics develops thinking skills and moral discernment that students apply to a range of practical situations in their personal, social and

working lives. Such skills might be as evident in the mechanic who discusses with the owner why a machine is not working and what should be done as it would be in a doctor diagnosing illness and discussing treatment options with a patient.

One of the effects of an outcomes focus was to downplay the study of the history and classics of philosophy and to place the primary focus on reasoning skills (Outcome 1) and conceptual inquiry (Outcome 2) and on the ways in which these can be applied in a variety of contexts (Outcome 3).

Measuring Outcomes

Measuring outcomes in all upper secondary courses became a source of controversy that played out, primarily, in the local news media. The controversy was not without foundation, however, as assessment originally did not allow for external examinations and secondary teachers were concerned to ensure that marks from different schools remained comparable.

Implementation

As noted above, the course was introduced in a difficult period, and yet its introduction went off smoothly.[4] The 'OBE (outcomes-based education) controversy' did nothing to delay the process.

In 2009, in the second year of its life, about 450 secondary students in about ten schools[5] were studying the Philosophy and Ethics course, up from 150 students in the previous year. In 2009 students sat the Tertiary Entrance Exam in Philosophy and Ethics for the first time.

The schools that have led the introduction include private and state schools whose students come from a range of socioeconomic backgrounds. However, to date, no Catholic schools have taken up the subject, and none has indicated any intention to do so. Catholic schools have chosen to support the religion course that they were instrumental in having approved.

An unexpected element of the story is that some of those leading the implementation process come from a background in the Dialogue Australasia Network (DAN), a non-denominational Christian organization.[6] DAN was established in 2002 by Peter Vardy of Heythrop College, London, and describes itself as 'an exciting and important initiative arising from a commitment to develop Values, Philosophy & Religious Studies with intellectual rigour and contemporary relevance in Australasian schools'.[7] In its 'five-strand' approach DAN contends, for example, that students need to be made aware of 'the tension between belief in a wholly good and all powerful God and the undoubted reality of evil' and that they 'need to be given the opportunity to think through the consequences of this tension in an intellectual framework that takes the issues seriously, whilst also encouraging freedom of thought'.[8] Taking this at face value, there is no obvious incompatibility between these approaches and that of the Lipman P4C tradition. However, the P4C tradition is more deeply embedded in the

Western Australian Philosophy and Ethics course and that tradition will provide a framework for the subject in non-Christian schools.

Resources and Teaching

A perennial problem for wholly new courses, as this course is, is the need for appropriate teaching materials. However, a local publisher, Impact Publishing, offered the authors of this article the chance to write three textbooks tailored to the needs of the course. These were completed in 2007–2008[9] (Millett & Tapper, 2007, 2008a, 2008b; see also Millett & Tapper, 2011). The books are written with the aim of combining a 'community of inquiry' approach with an introduction to philosophical ideas, arguments and methods.

A more basic problem is 'human resources'. The long neglect of philosophy in schools means that very few current teachers have training in the subject area. Only a handful of teachers in the state have philosophy degrees. A few hundred have taken introductory Level One courses run by APIS, but many of these teachers are at primary school level. Thus, the teaching of philosophy and ethics will of necessity fall to those teachers who have studied a little philosophy and who have an enthusiasm for the subject sufficient to motivate them to go through a difficult learning process. If student demand for the course continues to grow, it will soon outstrip the supply of teachers. How to increase that supply remains an unsolved problem, but also presents an opportunity for education and philosophy schools in universities.

The Wider Perspective

Philosophy was once a central part of the tradition of English and Scottish schooling, on which Australian educational traditions are largely based. It was also once part of the Catholic tradition, which forms an important segment of Australian schooling. Yet it has not been part of normal schooling for at least a century. The reintroduction of philosophy into Australian schools is a change worth viewing in a broad perspective. Here, we canvass four aspects of the change: philosophy is becoming accepted in the curriculum; it offers a way of teaching values; it is relevant to academic and non-academic levels of learning; and there is empirical evidence that it improves generic thinking skills.

First, there is the present status of philosophy in secondary schooling. Philosophy in Australian schools is 'in the process of coming in from the margins' (Millett, 2008) and has now been introduced into almost all secondary curricula, with the notable exception of New South Wales (NSW). This is summarized in Table 1.

Secondly, philosophy offers a way of teaching values. As we noted above, Western Australia is unusual in having a Curriculum Framework that incorporates an explicit set of 'core shared values' rather than something like the core values prescribed for NSW public schools, which refer to whole-of-school behaviours rather than specifically to the curriculum.[10] Typically, government schooling in Australia has been free, secular and compulsory, and in that formula 'secular' includes 'values neutral' in its implicit meaning. Philosophy, however, is a normative discipline. It involves the rational analysis of normative questions. This makes many of those from empirically

Table 1. Australia: Secondary philosophy courses, state by state.

State	Title	Cohort	Began	Pedagogy	Content	Outcomes focus	Course construction	External assessment
Western Australia	Philosophy and Ethics	Two final years, including vocational education students	2008	Community of inquiry required to be demonstrated as outcome	What is there? How do we know? How should we live?	Yes	Six units in three pairs	Yes
South Australia	Philosophy	Final years university entry	2003	Community of inquiry prescribed pedagogy	Key areas, e.g. ethics, epistemology, metaphysics; using film and popular texts	Yes	Two stages	Yes
Victoria	Philosophy	Final years, university entry	2001	Traditional, under review	Introduction to philosophical inquiry; philosophical issues in practice; the good life; mind and knowledge	Yes	Four units	Yes, two units
NSW	Distinction course in Philosophy	High achieving extension, final years	1994	Traditional	Metaphysics, epistemology, ethics	No	Two units	Yes, by University of New England
Queensland	Philosophy and Reason	Final years university entry	Long established but modified 2004	Traditional, but with request for 'vocally interactive classroom'	Critical reasoning, deductive logic, philosophy	Yes, criterion based	Three strands each with subunits	Yes
Tasmania	Religion and Philosophy	Final years	2006	Some community of inquiry	Five themes; possible to complete course by doing only religion components	Yes, criterion based	Four topics chosen from two of three sections	Yes

minded disciplines distinctly uncomfortable, and there is a deeply embedded fact/ value dichotomy that underpins this uneasiness. Philosophers, however, debate whether there is any rational basis for this uneasiness. Some think that facts and values can be sharply distinguished; others think the opposite. When the values are ethical values, the tension between these viewpoints is even further increased. But these are matters that philosophy knows how to discuss, even if the discussion does not end in agreement. The rational basis of ethics has been a central topic since the time of Socrates and Plato.

In an empiricist culture such as ours, 'values' tend to be—like a chronically misbehaving student—expelled from the curriculum. They are neither explicitly taught nor openly discussed. Yet this is incoherent, for three sorts of reason. One is that the school curriculum is already and undeniably value laden, at least as far as epistemic values are concerned. One cannot learn mathematics or history without learning to distinguish between false or worthless viewpoints and true and valuable viewpoints. Secondly, the classroom is a value-laden environment, and this is so for a much broader range of values. It cannot function, for instance, unless some kinds of behaviour are promoted and others discouraged. Thirdly, since one aim of Australian schooling is to prepare students for life in a democratic society, the values that apply (or should apply) in the wider society can reasonably be included in the curriculum. At the secondary level, this will include consideration of ways in which those values can be contested. This is already recognized in various ways in other disciplines, but philosophy makes these discussions explicit and central and focuses on the quality of the arguments, thus minimizing the risk of teachers imposing their selective visions on their students. One of the first rules of philosophy is that it is permissible, and even desirable, to disagree with the teacher, if one sees reason to do so. Of course, one can also disagree with one's fellow students.

Thirdly, philosophy is far from being a remote and academic subject fit only for high achievers intending to take an arts degree at university. Rather, philosophy in classes using the community of inquiry approach is a practical activity that helps students to understand, evaluate and engage with their world. It helps students to deal more effectively with disagreement and provides strategies to deal with issues that cannot be addressed simply by appeal to the senses or to some rule or law. Philosophy teaches transferable skills and makes a unique contribution to a student's understanding of his or her self. Philosophy aims to empower students to flourish in a world of increasing complexity of not just new problems, but new categories of problems.

Fourthly, strong empirical research now backs up strong claims about the value of philosophy in schools (Millett & Tapper, 2011). The best research evidence comes from Clackmannanshire, Scotland, where Keith Topping and Steve Trickey studied the effects of collaborative philosophical inquiry on students in 18 primary schools (Trickey & Topping, 2004, 2006, 2007; Topping & Trickey, 2007a, 2007b):

- A whole population of children gained on average 6 standard points on a measure of cognitive abilities after 16 months of weekly enquiry (1 hour per week).

- Pupils and teachers perceived significant gains in communication, confidence, concentration, participation and social behaviour following 6 months of enquiry.
- Pupils doubled their occurrence of supporting their views with reasons over a 6 month period.
- Teachers doubled their use of open-ended questions over a 6 month period.
- When pupils left primary school they did not have any further enquiry opportunities yet their improved cognitive abilities were still sustained 2 years into secondary school.
- Pupils increased their level of participation in classroom discussion by half as much again following 6 months of weekly enquiry. (Sutcliffe, in UNESCO, 2011, pp. 53–54)

We should perhaps underline the point that 'communication, confidence, concentration, participation and social behaviour' all improved where students learned to participate in disciplined but democratic discussion. Philosophy does not bring only intellectual gains.

Another study, a meta-analysis of 18 studies of the cognitive effectiveness of the P4C approach, carried out by Garcia-Moriyon, Colom, Lora, and Rivas (2004), concluded that 'the implementation of P4C led to an improvement of students' reasoning skills of more than half a standard deviation'. This amounts to a gain of about seven IQ points. The researchers observed that 'The result is especially impressive if we note that P4C was never applied for more than one school year in all the studies reviewed' (Garcia-Moriyon et al., 2004, pp. 19, 21).

Conclusion

The Western Australian senior school curriculum is an example of how a proven pedagogy can be built into a curriculum in such a way that students, by working within this pedagogy, can achieve outcomes intended to make them good citizens capable of clear, considered and collaborative thinking.

Despite its effectiveness, philosophy in schools has suffered in part because it has not been adequately scoped and sequenced so that students are able to build their philosophical capacity in ways analogous to the ways their capacities in numeracy, literacy and scientific understanding are built across the whole of their schooling. With the weight of evidence showing significant and measurable improvements in cognitive and social elements for students who learn philosophical methods through collaborative classroom inquiry, it is time that philosophy became more fully enmeshed in school life and time that pre-service training for teachers included philosophical methods and appropriate pedagogy.

Ethics Approval

Interviews for this article were conducted with ethics approval from the Curtin University Human Research Ethics Committee, approval number RD-34-10.

Notes

1. For an earlier discussion of the state philosophy courses, see Millett (2006).
2. The course syllabus can be accessed at http://www.curriculum.wa.edu.au/internet/ Senior_Secondary/Courses/Philosophy_and_Ethics
3. http://www.curriculum.wa.edu.au/internet/Years_K10/Curriculum_Framework (accessed November 2010).
4. Critics of OBE, many of whom joined the 'PLATO' lobby (people lobbying against teaching outcomes), commonly feared that declining educational standards would follow from the new curriculum approach. But it is not easy to argue that a subject as notoriously difficult as philosophy would have the effect of lowering school standards. In 2007, a few of the PLATO protagonists did in fact argue that philosophy was *too difficult* even for upper secondary school students. They took up this line of argument in ignorance of the 'philosophy in schools' movement. When the work of Dewey and Lipman was drawn to their attention, one or two tried to contend that this was not 'real philosophy', as measured by the yardsticks of Kant and Hegel. However, the argument died a natural death and had no impact on the implementation process. This argument took place on the forum of the PLATO website, http://www.platowa.com/, in 2007. The website is no longer active and the argument can no longer be accessed.
5. Australind Senior High School, Carey Baptist College, Christ Church Grammar School, Gilmore College, Hale School, Mt Lawley Senior High School, St Hilda's Anglican School for Girls, Perth College, Perth Modern School and Willetton Senior High School.
6. We have in mind Matthew Wills at Hale School (formerly DAN director) and Dominic Hodnett at Christ Church Grammar School. In 2007, with APIS member Leanne Rucks, Matthew Wills launched the 'Philosothon', now a rapidly growing annual interschool 'community of inquiry' event that is at once both competitive and cooperative. See the website, http://www.philosothon.org/
7. See DAN's website, http://www.dialogueaustralasia.org/
8. See the 'five strands' at http://www.dialogueaustralasia.org/?page_id=23
9. The publisher's website is http://www.impactpublishing.com.au/catalogue.php?groupid=32
10. http://www.schools.nsw.edu.au/studentsupport/studentwellbeing/values/core/index.ph0070

References

Dewey, J. (1966). *Democracy and education: An introduction to the philosophy of education.* New York: Free Press. (Original work published 1916).

Dewey, J. (1933). *How we think. A restatement of the relation of reflective thinking to the educative process* (rev. ed.). Boston: D. C. Heath. (Original work published 1910).

Dewey, J. (1957). *Reconstruction in philosophy.* Boston: Beacon Press. (Original work published 1920).

Garcia-Moriyon, F. F., Colom, R., Lora, S., & Rivas, M. V. (2004). Evaluation of Philosophy for Children: A program of learning thinking skills. *Thinking: The Journal of Philosophy for Children, 17,* 17–26.

Lipman, M. (1974). *Harry Stottlemeier's discovery.* New York: Columbia University Press.

Millett, S. (2006). Philosophy in upper secondary school: An example from Western Australia. In H. W. Kam (Ed.), *Philosophy in schools: Developing a community of inquiry.* Report on the proceedings of the conference (pp. 87–99). Singapore: Singapore Teachers' Union.

Millett, S. (2008). Coming in from the margins: Teaching philosophy in Australian schools. *Thinking, 19.*

Millett, S., & Tapper, A. (2007). *Philosophy and ethics. A resource for units 2A and 2B.* Perth: Impact Publishing.

Millett, S., & Tapper, A. (2008a). *Philosophy and ethics. A resource for units 1A and 1B*. Perth: Impact Publishing.

Millett, S., & Tapper, A. (2008b). *Philosophy and ethics. A resource for units 3A and 3B*. Perth: Impact Publishing.

Millett, S., & Tapper, A. (2011). Benefits of collaborative philosophical inquiry in schools. *Educational Philosophy and Theory, 44*(5), 546–547.

Sutcliffe, R. (2011). In *UNESCO High level regional meeting on the teaching of philosophy*, February 14–16, Milan (pp. 53–54). Retrieved from www.unesco.org

Topping, K. J., & Trickey, S. (2007a). Collaborative philosophical enquiry for school children: Cognitive effects at 10–12 years. *British Psychological Society*.

Topping, K. J., & Trickey, S. (2007b). Collaborative philosophical state inquiry for schoolchildren: Cognitive gains at 2-year follow-up. *British Journal of Educational Psychology, 77*, 787–796.

Trickey, S., & Topping, K. J. (2004). Philosophy for children: A systematic review. *Research Papers in Education, 19*, 363–378.

Trickey, S., & Topping, K. J. (2006). Collaborative philosophical inquiry for school children: Socio-emotional effects at 11 to 12 years. *School Psychology International, 27*, 599–614.

Trickey, S., & Topping, K. J. (2007). Collaborative philosophical enquiry for school children: Cognitive effects at 10–12 years. *British Journal of Educational Psychology, 77*, 271–288.

Vygotsky, L. S. (1978). Mind in society: The development of higher psychological processes. M. Cole, V. John-Steiner, S. Scribner & E. Souberman (Eds.). Cambridge, MA: Harvard University Press.

Western Australia Curriculum Council. (2002). *Our youth, our future: Post-compulsory education review: Summary of the directions endorsed by the Western Australian government/Curriculum Council*. Osborne Park, WA: Curriculum Council.

That's Not For Our Kids: The strange death of philosophy and ethics in a low socioeconomic secondary school

GREG THOMPSON & TOMAŽ LAŠIČ

School of Education, Murdoch University

Abstract

This article reflects on the successes and failures of a new Philosophy and Ethics course in a low socioeconomic context in Perth, Western Australia, with the eventual demise of the subject in the school at the end of 2010. We frame this reflection within Deleuzian notions of geophilosophy to advocate for a Philosophy and Ethics that is informed by nomadic thought, as this offers a critical freedom for students to transform themselves and their society and suggests practical ways both of overcoming the prejudices which led to its demise and of student reluctance to engage in open discussion in class. We consider the demise of the course a 'missed opportunity' because it had so much potential to be transformative of student subjectivities in schools.

Introduction

This article focuses on the implementation and teaching of the Philosophy and Ethics course at Marri College,[1] a public co-educational high school in Perth, Western Australia. It charts the rise and demise of the subject, the successes and challenges over a two-year period from 2009 to 2010. There is no happy ending as the course, offered first in 2009 and restricted in 2010, was not offered in 2011. In the spirit of geophilosophy, this article will chart the experiences of teaching Philosophy and Ethics in a 'challenging' school context. We use Deleuzian analytics to suggest that while the subject could offer so much to students, there are significant challenges in making the curriculum and pedagogy relevant and useful to students from low socioeconomic backgrounds.

Since studying a unit together in contemporary educational philosophy the authors have embarked on a series of collaborations that seek to problematize the 'accident of history' that is mass compulsory schooling. At that time, one of us was working as a teacher in Philosophy and Ethics at Marri College, while the other was critically researching student subjectivities at Marri College. This is a shared article that explores those experiences and conversations and our interest in the promise of Philosophy and Ethics for students from low socioeconomic backgrounds.

Philosophy and Ethics fascinated the students at Marri College because they saw it as giving them the opportunity to wrestle with ideas that were the 'stuff' of their worlds. We approached Philosophy and Ethics as a vehicle to problematize and challenge the stuff of their world, because: 'once one steps outside what's been thought before, once one steps outside what's familiar and reassuring … thinking becomes, as Foucault puts it, a "perilous act" whose first victim is oneself' (Deleuze, 1990/1995, p. 103). We are strongly opposed to the single-minded application of instrumental or vocational orientations to the curriculum that we have found deeply embedded within many institutions dealing with people who live within low socioeconomic areas (Reid, 2009, p. 11). Smyth, Angus, Down, and McInerney (2008) have identified schools in similar contexts to Marri College as being representative of 'excluded communities'. These 'patterns of exclusion bear down on schools' and one of the effects of this is that many of these schools adopt a curriculum that can best be considered as preparation for work (Smyth et al., 2008). In this context, Philosophy and Ethics could be the kind of subject that disrupts the reproduction of disadvantage because it challenges the vocational determinism so often found in schools in lower socioeconomic areas. Smyth et al. (2008, pp. 70–71) argue that bringing student lives into the curriculum is a strategy to combat the alienation and irrelevance that many students experience in schools.

Marri is a school whose curriculum indicates a strong vocational orientation, with a subsequent lack of those subjects traditionally seen as appropriate for academic, tertiary-study bound students. There is increasing evidence that this vocational curriculum is dividing state education into a dual system 'in which working class kids were streamed into vocational classes and away from academic courses and "powerful knowledges"' (Smyth, Down, & McInerney, 2010, p. 138). We saw an opportunity for Philosophy and Ethics to be taught in such a way as to acknowledge and value the students' distinct experience, their cultural capital, to turn them on to the inventive, creative and experimental becomings that we see as potentially transformative and emancipatory (Colebrook, 2002, p. 2; Semetsky & Lovat, 2008; Semetsky, 2008). Our aims were political, yet open and pragmatic. We saw philosophy for its potential not to direct but to 'donate a gift of potential for use in other people's lives and projects. Philosophy is a doing, and it acts for change' (Massumi, 2010, p. 3).

In 2008, a key school leader's first reaction to the idea of offering a Philosophy and Ethics course in 2009 was: 'Philosophy? That's not for our kids. You can give it a try but I don't think you will get enough kids to run a class in that [subject]'. With some strategic 'selling' that centred on 29 open-ended questions that related directly to their experience,[2] Philosophy and Ethics began as a combined 11/12 class of 25 students studying at the 1A/1B non-tertiary entrance examination (TEE) level. This made it the biggest humanities subject offered at Marri College in its first year. Its demise some three years later represents, to us, a 'missed opportunity': contextual, systemic and programmatic.

Theory and Literature

Here, we utilize the philosophical method of 'geophilosophy' of Deleuze and Guattari to unmask the relationship between thought, 'territory and the earth' (Deleuze & Guattari, 1991/1996, p. 85). For Deleuze and Guattari, philosophical thought concerns movement within mapped terrains that revolves around a triple connection or three movements: finding territory or territories, abandoning or leaving them (deterritorializing) and then re-creating them in slightly different forms (reterritorializing) (Deleuze & Guattari, 1991/1996, pp. 67–68). For Deleuze and Guattari, philosophy should be 'done' rather than be 'content to reflect, pronouncing upon the world from a disengaged posture of explanatory description of judgemental prescription' (Massumi, 2010, p. 3). It is this pragmatic aspect that explained to us how we could best engage with the contextual uniqueness of our students; their experiences, narratives and expectations.

Philosophy and Ethics is both a territory itself and a concept that forms part of the terrain of education, as 'concepts link up with each other, support one another, coordinate their contours, articulate their respective problems, and belong to the same philosophy, even if they have different history' (Deleuze & Guattari, 1991/1996, p. 18). In other words, Philosophy and Ethics, its syllabus, rationale, implementation, pedagogy and assessment, is part of the wider world of competing and contradictory discourses that shape mass compulsory schooling (Hunter, 1994; Symes & Preston, 1997; Popkewitz, 1998; Ball, 2008). So, Philosophy and Ethics is not valueless or divorced from its context: it is part of the wider milieu, informed as much by both those competing and contradictory discourses that we could loosely term the philosophies of education; highly contested, contextual and productive.

Philosophy and Ethics came into being in the relationships, connections and becomings valued by the corporate and neoliberal context of education within Australia and the connection being made within those landscapes. We do not see young people as victims of their socioeconomic narratives; we see them as ideally situated to think in new ways about the world or 'territories' in which they move. For us, this is about students unmasking how they could be freer within their territories. Philosophy and Ethics seemed to engage with thought in a way few (if any) school subjects allowed.

As expected, there was a continual tension and conflict with corporate discourses of education that currently seem to hold much sway within contemporary philosophies of education that support a performative culture (Hey, 2002; Ball, 2003; Thompson, 2010). Partly, this can be thought of as the tension between nomadic and state orientations played out in education. For Deleuze, nomadism is the 'smooth space' between 'two striated spaces' (Deleuze & Guattari, 1980/2005, pp. 384–385). Nomadism is characterized by dynamic, unknown landscapes that create new concepts, new forms of flow or movement in deterritorializing ways through previously controlled or regulated landscapes. This smooth space is caught between statism or sedentary spaces, which is that method of enclosing territories within rules, practices, truths and dominant discourses (Deleuze & Guattari, 1980/2005). This means advocating for 'dynamic and evolving character of philosophical contexts versus their having forever-fixed and eternal meanings' (Semetsky, 2008, p. viii).

In essence, this was our project: to use Philosophy and Ethics as a vehicle for young people to challenge some truths about themselves and their worlds that they had previously been educated to accept in often unsophisticated and uncritical ways. We wanted them to experience 'nomadic movements' (Massumi, 2010, p. 7) uncontained within the boundaries of existing identities and unregulated by the economy of the normal, gridded channels of circulation (e.g. school, syllabus, Department of Education policies). Nomadism offers opportunities for young people to engage with rhizomatic knowledge, concerned as it is with multiplicities, lines and strata (Deleuze & Guattari, 1980/2005, p. 4). Rhizomatic knowledge is a multiplicity, a plane of possibilities and potentials in contrast to the Western 'tree' where knowledge is organized and hierarchical. The rhizome is of the smooth space of the nomad, rather than the cultivated, enclosed space of the state.

However, we recognize that we work within limits imposed by the education systems: the cultivated, enclosed spaces of education that have come to dominate mass, compulsory schooling. Advocating critical thought within the striated spaces of schools challenges many individuals' conceptions of what education should be. At a theoretical level, nomadism and statism are not rigid binaries that should be valued one over the other. That we prefer nomadism is significant but, as Deleuze and Guattari point out, it is about dosages. 'Staying stratified—organised, signified, subjected—is not the worst that can happen; the worst that can happen is if you throw the strata into demented or suicidal collapse, which brings them back down on us heavier than ever' (Deleuze & Guattari, 1980/2005, p. 161). We see nomadism in pragmatic terms; it is about assisting young people to use the stuff of their worlds in new ways rather than overthrowing the corporate culture of schools that we find so challenging, and we see Philosophy and Ethics as potentially nomadic (and therefore deterritorializing) within the enclosed terrain of the corporation of education. And it is this potential, once realized and made possible, that can serve as a catalyst for these students to (re)invent themselves and shape their becomings as members of various communities in freer ways.

About the Site

Marri College is a public, co-educational high school that operates within the city of Marri, formed from an amalgamation of two smaller high schools in 1996 as part of the Western Australian government's rationalization of schools. In 2009 there were approximately 547 students at the college from Years 8 to 12 (Education Department of Western Australia, 2010). In 2009, the attendance rate at Marri was 83%, significantly lower than the state average of 88.0% (Education Department of Western Australia). In 2009 16 students, representing 32% of the Year 12 cohort, studied the required number of TEE subjects to qualify for direct tertiary entrance (Education Department of Western Australia). Only one student achieved a scaled score of 75+ in their TEE. Sixteen per cent of the student population were classified as Aboriginal, and the school ran specific programmes for Aboriginal students such as Aboriginal School Based Traineeships in conjunction with the Education Department (Education Department of Western Australia, 2010). In 2009 NAPLAN testing, Year 9 students at Marri scored significantly lower than the national average in the areas of numeracy, reading, writing, spelling, and grammar (Education Department of Western Australia).

The Strange Death of Philosophy and Ethics

Enrolments in Year 11 and 12 subjects in the Society and Environment-based courses at Marri College were in a steady decline in 2007 and 2008. This tended to mirror the experience of many schools in Western Australia, at least partly explained by structural changes in the calculation of a student's Tertiary Entrance Rank. In response to this decline, many hours in the Humanities Department at Marri were spent on thinking how these subjects could be made more appealing to students. One strategy to reverse the trend was to offer a wider variety of courses in an 'expo' format in late 2008 and let students in Year 10 vote on which courses they most wanted to study. The school administration decided that the three most popular courses chosen by the students would be offered in 2009. Philosophy and Ethics was among the three voted favourites.

At the start of 2009, Philosophy and Ethics 1A/1B course had 22 enrolled students, the highest number of enrolments in any of the three Society and Environment-based courses. Owing to its popularity amongst Year 12 students, the decision was made to offer the course as a combined Year 11/Year 12 class. By the end of 2009 another four students had changed subjects to study Philosophy and Ethics. In comparison, the course with the second highest enrolment in this learning area had 14 students. Student feedback suggested that the main reasons for choosing Philosophy and Ethics were that it was new and interesting, it seemed relevant to their lives, and they were motivated by the promise of exploring their thinking in their own terms as well as grounding some of their anxieties such as success, friendship and love. There was also a feeling that it would be interesting as it was taught by a teacher who was known for creative, innovative pedagogical approaches to traditional subjects offered in the school curriculum.

It was clear that students engaged with the content that they saw as 'speaking' to their worlds. Part of the subtext to the syllabus is the idea of interrogating the discourses of the happy life that dominate, often in uncritical ways, the aspirations and understandings of these students (Curriculum Council, 2007). There were many occasions where these explorations had unplanned benefits, such as when a student explained that his relationship with his father had improved because of their discussions about what constituted a 'happy life'.

In addition, students often reported appreciating the freedom to pause, think and express themselves. For many this was a new experience. They could not recall many, or any, other times either in their school life or in their life outside school when they felt that their thoughts and opinions were valued. This became increasingly important as many of these students wrestled with other people and problems as they moved through their schooling. For example, a gay, anti-religious student and a group of strongly religious Christian students had a chance to speak to each other very openly about homosexuality and ideas of sin in an honest way.

Students began asking philosophical questions outside the classroom: 'Sir, what is normal?', 'Is school just like a habit some people get good at?', 'How real is friendship online?', 'If thinking can make you really upset, why do it? That's not happiness is it?' These were just some of the questions asked by students studying Philosophy and Ethics, often randomly in the school yard, sometimes during a class in a different subject, sometimes online during and after school hours using the Internet. This illustrates that the Philosophy and Ethics course was both challenging and potentially transformative as it impacted on the ways they saw and understood their worlds.

This point was further reinforced by teaching colleagues who provided similar, positive reports about the impact of Philosophy and Ethics courses in their own classes. For example, after approximately one semester three English teachers separately reported that they could point out which of the students in their class also studied Philosophy and Ethics. They had clearly improved in their expression, and in their confidence and mastery in thinking critically about the content of their English course. The coordinator of a very successful mentoring programme for Indigenous students reported how the two Aboriginal students in her programme enjoyed Philosophy and Ethics not just for the novelty and variety of discussions but because it was one of the very few places at the school where they could openly and confidently talk about the issues of race and contemporary issues affecting Indigenous students.

However, these positive experiences were offset by inevitable tensions implicit in contemporary education. One of the challenges was in thinking about how we could shape and reshape the traditional 'enclosed spaces' of Philosophy and Ethics in ways that would prove more accessible and educative for our students. In particular, the student cohort at Marri College studying Philosophy and Ethics was diverse in terms of academic achievement (from a Year 12 Academic Award winner to migrants with poor English) and ethnic background (11 white Australian-born students, three Aboriginal students, two black South African students and nine Filipino migrant students who had migrated and had English as a second language, an unusually high concentration of these students in one class). This was a culturally diverse group, and along with this came a number of challenges in working with this diversity. For example, most Filipino students found the notion of disagreeing with other students or a teacher challenging. As one of our aims was to decentre the relations of power in the traditional teacher–student relationship, this required careful thought. We decided to explore new technologies as a tool to facilitate moving beyond 'disciplined' thought to create opportunities for more nomadic thinking. Thoughtful use of Moodle, an online learning management system, was an innovative approach to learning in Philosophy and Ethics.

Moodle is an online platform which allows teachers and students to store and share digitized content. Students and teachers can communicate, evaluate and collaborate at any time from anywhere via the Internet through Moodle. Moodle was used by students to access key course materials such as syllabus documents, key readings, links to useful sites, stimulus images and videos. However, Moodle was of most benefit as an interactive tool, allowing collaboration and the exchange of views within and beyond the space and time of the class(room). Moodle used tools such as wikis (collaboratively edited documents), blogs (online reflective journals) and student-created glossaries. Online forums played a particularly important part in this decentring of those traditional and vocational discourses of schooling at Marri College. They were frequently used by students to reflect, question, expand on, explore, contest and problematize 'common-sense' knowledge that they had previously taken for granted or may have felt they lacked the positionality to critique. The use of Moodle substantially altered the landscape of the classroom in which learning took place.

Moodle forums offered a number of different benefits. Many students found it difficult to engage in discussion or debate in the class. This may have been because of a fear of failure, cultural understandings of shame, peer pressure, poor English language skills or group dynamics. Forums were a chance to 'level' with others without raised voices or being cut off by more outwardly dominant students. Forums gave all students the chance to take their time asking questions, constructing answers and critiquing the responses of others at any time. The easy insertion of hyperlinks, images and media made substantiation and explanation of claims a lot easier while offering opportunities for students to extend their critical understanding. Sometimes this was teacher directed, but often it was students who communicated to other students the need for more critical thinking. One of the hallmarks of this process was that many students became skilled at challenging the assertions of others by asking for proof or evidence to support their claims; this was a challenge to traditional methods of teaching philosophy where analytical traditions are often taught first and ideas and concepts come later. Moodle was used to stimulate, guide and evaluate conversations, and it was possible to gather important personal insights about students that arguably would not have surfaced in classroom discussions (e.g. certain cultural and career expectations) but were freely supplied by students online, often through a private channel with the teacher. Blogs gave an opportunity for students to reflect individually on their learning and the connections between the Philosophy and Ethics course and their daily, lived experiences. Wikis were a wonderful opportunity for students to negotiate and collaborate on a piece of writing. Often this involved negotiation, conflict resolution and peer tutoring as the students wrestled with complex ideas and opinions.

Perhaps the most important aspect of using Moodle was the possibility for all students to 'unbind' conversations from those 'prescribed' by the teacher and start conversations they were interested in by themselves, then generate and nurture interest in others by replying and developing threads. It is 'always by rhizome that desire moves and produces' (Deleuze & Guattari, 1980/2005, p. 14). Through the forums the students exhibited a desire to learn, to question, to challenge and to think, which grew over time. This rhizomatic exploration of concepts was far more creative and innovative than anything that could have been generated by the teacher alone. In addition, the students grew with the rhizomes, as they were given opportunities to become both knowledgeable and powerful within the context of their study. We would argue that this growth had the potential to shift the focus in the course from epistemological to ontological, as students became increasingly concerned with their self and their place in their world, in the context of normalized concepts often found in schools such as 'success' or 'authority'.

But not everything went well in Philosophy and Ethics. One of the major challenges in teaching Philosophy and Ethics at Marri College was to do with the expectations of the curriculum and many of the hidden assumptions enshrined within its pages. The first of these was the community of inquiry (COI), which was one of the key requirements of Philosophy and Ethics course. Basically, a COI is a pedagogic tool to engage students in verbally interrogating and arguing in an inquiring mode about key concepts and ideas. As such, it privileges those students who come from a background that is immersed in verbal debate and have a firm grasp of English to be able to structure coherent and rational responses. It assumes that these students will understand academic arguments and criticism, or an explanation that this modality can be learned quickly. In the context of the students at Marri College this was not the case. Throughout the course, many attempts were made, and strategies employed, to engage students with COI, particularly the difference between exploratory, listening, common-ground seeking dialogue and the more combative, competitive debate. Students often said they liked the idea of COI in its dialogue format but despite changing formats to improve participation (small groups, smaller focus, flexible topic choices, role plays, more teacher-led facilitation) COI very rarely developed into anything more than sessions of long silences and painful 'extraction' of questions and ideas by the teacher. Participation was usually restricted to a handful of the more confident class members. Students often expressed the wish to take part in win–lose debates instead of engaging in dialogue, suggesting that they were far more familiar with the adversarial form of knowledge, and this competitive aspect was part of the landscape they viewed as 'normal' (Thompson, 2010). While there was some minor improvement in COI activities, the forums and other online activities were far more successful in engaging students in dialogue and debate.

While the programme was carefully mapped out at the start of the year to cover the content and assessment requirements set up by Curriculum Council, we simply had to skip several smaller sections or approximately 15–20% of syllabus content in total. The two most common reasons for this were the poor English language skills of a disproportionately high number of students with English as a second language (nearly one half of the class) and the wish and willingness of students to explore those topics that they saw as important or relevant to their lives. We were left with the constant dilemma of forgoing depth of thought and engagement for the prescribed coverage of content, particularly the seemingly more 'technical' and less attractive aspects of the course for the students such as the analytical rules of argument and logical fallacies. We found that students engaged with the big ideas approach more in line with 'continental' philosophy rather than the prescriptive and argumentative approach consistent with the 'analytical' tradition. As a result, we prioritized activities and content that allowed the 'big ideas' rather than focus on disciplined and disciplining ways of thinking. This is not to say that we ignored the 'thinking tools' of philosophy: we simply used them in the context that that was most meaningful to the students.

We believe that a significant part of the challenge of teaching Philosophy and Ethics at Marri College concerned a misunderstanding of what philosophy actually was. In the minds of various members of the school community, Philosophy and Ethics was seen as an elitist subject that offered little practical assistance for students from low socioeconomic backgrounds. The reaction 'That's not for our kids', we explain as being representative of the ways that schools (and members of school communities) idealize attributes and characteristics in terms of the grand narratives of class, gender and ethnicity (McLeod & Yates, 2006; Wetherall, 2009; Thompson, 2010). It is these normalizing judgements that Foucault argued could be found within schools as 'a sort of apparatus of uninterrupted examination' that has as its purpose the disciplining and self-disciplining of the subjectivities of young people (Foucault, 1975/1991, p. 186).

The administration of the school, however, always appeared uncomfortable with Philosophy and Ethics being at Marri. This wariness manifested itself in various ways such as the administration warning the staff in the humanities learning area against offering courses like Philosophy and Ethics owing to the potential for scaling variations in TEE/WACE exams.[3] Instead, they were advised to offer more 'settled' and traditional courses such as Geography and History. Despite the administration acknowledging that Philosophy and Ethics in 2009 was a successful course, a decision was made not to offer it in 2010. The reasoning for this was never clearly explained to either staff or students. The course was enthusiastically supported by the current students, and many students in lower grades spoke of being excited at the possibility of studying Philosophy and Ethics. While there was some resistance from the staff, there were also many teachers who supported the subject as they saw the benefits in their own class. Ultimately, the school offered Philosophy and Ethics in 2010, but only as a 2A/2B course to Year 12 students, with no Year 11 enrolments or courses at 1A/1B level. This effectively meant the slow, strange death of the subject.

In 2010 the course had only 14 students, two of whom would sit a Philosophy and Ethics WACE end-of-year examination. This required the new teacher to exhaustively cover the content for fear of missing something that would disadvantage the two students. As a result, we understand that there was a gradual erosion of student interest as the content became more superficially covered and the assessment tasks became more complex and less transferable. The grades of the students, particularly those not planning to sit the examination, fell. This became part of the self-fulfilling prophecy: at the end of the course the results probably supported the view that Philosophy and Ethics was not for our kids. Philosophy and Ethics was not offered as a subject choice in 2011.

Beyond the challenges presented by the student cohort themselves, neither the administration nor staff members across the school were comfortable with the meaningful scrutiny and critical inquiry fundamental to Philosophy and Ethics. When students challenge the 'comfortable' assumptions played out in schools they disrupt notions of authority or normality. These challenges often meant that for the students, one of the greatest challenges was escaping the(ir) 'schooled' subjectivities to move across the enclosed terrains of their thought in freer (nomad) ways. For example, we found that over the course of the year, students became more and more fixated on the examination, and expressed a resultant desire for certainty—concrete answers that they could rely on. Within schools there is a myriad of competing and contradictory discourses that coalesce into hegemonic visions concerning what education is and should be. In a school in a low socioeconomic setting, we found that there were significant structural and pedagogic incentives for the reproduction of the *status quo* rather than the transformation of schooling to become more flexible, dynamic and creative (Symes & Preston, 1997).

The hegemony of smooth space was exacerbated by the lack of support offered at the systemic level for this new subject. Other than a handful of philosophy units at undergraduate and postgraduate level, a keen interest in Philosophy For Children (P4C), educational philosophy and critical thought, the teacher did not have a formal certification or extensive training in philosophy. This could be understood within the context of the impoverishment of philosophy in undergraduate teaching degrees, and many teachers would report a similar difficulty. One-day pre-course workshop/professional development (PD) sessions offered by the Curriculum Council in 2008 clashed with other compulsory PD courses and were directed at the more 'advanced' streams of 2A/2B and 3A/3B. The attempt to set up mentoring relationships for less experienced teachers was fairly unproductive, largely because the mentor assigned had little knowledge and experience of teaching in a low socioeconomic setting and offered very limited advice, aimed mostly at catering for the 'elite' students. The Curriculum Council Officer was extremely helpful but difficult to access. It was very difficult to see a live example, even a video clip, of a COI working in another school. Networking events were occasionally publicized by the Curriculum Council Officer, but without the support of the school in terms of funding and/or leave, more extensive training, networking, collegial sharing and enrichment across the state remained a wish.

Discussion

For us, the Philosophy and Ethics course at Marri College presented a number of challenges, but also a number of opportunities. To paraphrase Deleuze and Guattari, we worried that the institutional and systemic drive to 'do' Philosophy and Ethics would mean that students had little time to think (Deleuze & Guattari, 1991/1996, p. 1). What became increasingly clear to us was the ways that the landscape of education 'gridded' the possibilities inherent within the course. It is this gridding that maps the terrain through which the individual moves, communicating possibilities and normalities, orchestrating connections and always enmeshing the individual within complex systems and games of power. There is an inherent tension in advocating critical thought within an institution that has become increasingly dominated by philosophies and orientations that are predominantly anti-creative. This tension forms part of what we now know as the modern school, explained by Hunter (1994) as the clash between historically competing visions. These contradictory visions comprise the vision of the school as a form of vocational training exemplified by 'discipline, rote learning and inculcation of subaltern moral values' set against the vision of education as 'democratically organised and dedicated to human emancipation' (Hunter, 1994, p. xi). The failure of Philosophy and Ethics needs to be understood in the broader context of ongoing education debates and policies that have increasingly come to value globalized and performative systemic and schooling cultures that reproduce the social stratification so visible at Marri College.

One of the deepest lines that gridded the terrain at Marri concerned the conception of the aptitude and capabilities of the student who came from a low socioeconomic background. This was a key feature of our experience at Marri College, the positioning of these young people within highly vocational discourses that assumed that they were destined to be come certain types of citizens—retail workers, tradespeople, manual labourers—and, as such, subjects like Philosophy and Ethics were not of their world. Schools are reproducers of disadvantage (and advantage) rather than social levellers despite the rhetoric and, we believe, best intentions of those associated with schools (Symes & Preston, 1997). Partly, what we contested was the deficit model often applied to students from low socioeconomic backgrounds. Instead, we saw them as advantaged in certain ways and sought through our pedagogy (such as the use of Moodle) to advantage their unique positionality within the context of schooling. What we found most difficult was that many of these young people are so trapped through their subjectivation that they found it difficult to move through their terrains in new ways. This movement takes time to learn, and we feel that just when they were beginning to become more dynamic and creative, the course was effectively terminated by the school.

In part, this reinforces research that suggests that because of the terrains in which people move, they find it incredibly difficult to escape the faces that they wear (Deleuze & Guattari, 1980/2005; O'Sullivan, 2006; Thompson, 2010). The students were suspicious of attempts to ask them to interrogate their schooling (even though they were highly critically aware about many things due to their disadvantage) because of the way they had been positioned as disempowered within their schooling. Our experiences of teaching Philosophy and Ethics increasingly led us to question the role of the school in the 'making of the self', particularly the 'low socioeconomic self' (McLeod & Yates, 2006). We also began to increasingly interrogate the curriculum as a reterritorializing terrain, rather than the vehicle through which we could assist young people in examining their selves and their worlds.

One of the most significant successes of Philosophy and Ethics at Marri College lay in the use of alternative modes of pedagogy, particularly through the thoughtful use of technologies such as Moodle. Ironically, online technologies allowed students to engage in more embodied and authentic ways with ideas and concepts that had often appeared foreign and impractical for their worlds. Online technologies also enabled a shift in the relations of power towards an epistemology emphasizing rhizomatic thought. The impact of this will be difficult to assess; we wonder whether these students' understanding of this potential will become increasingly reterritorialized as they finish their schooling.

If Philosophy and Ethics wants to become a subject that is studied in a wide range of schools (as we would argue it should), not only should more support structures be put in place, but it must be carefully evaluated in the light of who it privileges, in terms of the curriculum, the pedagogy presumed and the ways in which it is implemented and administered at a systemic level.

Conclusion

This article has focused on the experiences of teaching Philosophy and Ethics in a secondary school within a low socioeconomic area. Contextual and systemic tensions in implementing this subject unfortunately contributed to the demise of Philosophy and Ethics. Our positive experiences centred on the enthusiasm and aptitude that many of these students showed for this subject. We found that new technologies presented many rich learning experiences for the students that allowed a critical awareness of their worlds. The rhizomatic opportunities for these students to unmask and interrogate the common-sense assumptions of their worlds were highly successful in the short term, although we are unsure as to how this will be maintained over time given the institutional inclination to endorse more traditional approaches to epistemology.

However, these successes were largely offset by powerful discourses. Traditional disciplinary approaches to knowledge, normalized constructions (largely vocational) of what is appropriate for the students at Marri College and the wider performative culture of education inevitably clashed with our emphasis on critical and problematizing thought. Unfortunately, this divided the students and the administration, the many students who wanted the subject to continue and the school administration that resisted or could not see its potential. We argue that it is this critical approach that attracted the students, yet it was also this approach that seemed to harden the opposition of members of the school community. Ultimately, Philosophy and Ethics will not be offered at Marri in the future, and we see this as a missed opportunity, not just for the growth of the subject, but for the lives of the students themselves.

Notes

1. Not its real name. Specific details about lower socioeconomic status are not given in order to avoid identification through departmental records.
2. Questions such as: Should everyone be treated the same after making a mistake? When is it OK to reveal a secret? Can jokes hurt if they are just jokes?
3. Until 2007 students studying for tertiary entrance studied Tertiary Entrance Examination (TEE) subjects. In 2008 this was changed, with TEE replaced by the Western Australian Certificate of Education (WACE) courses of study.

References

Ball, S. (2003). The teacher's soul and the terrors of performativity. *Journal of Education Policy*, *18*, 215–228.

Ball, S. (2008). *The education debate*. Bristol: Policy Press.

Colebrook, C. (2002). *Gilles Deleuze*. London: Routledge.

Curriculum Council. (2007). *Philosophy and ethics*. Retrieved July 18, 2010, from http://www.curriculum.wa.edu.au/internet/Senior_Secondary/Courses/WACE_Courses/Philosophy_and_Ethics

Deleuze, G. (1995). Postscript on control societies. In G. Deleuze (Ed.), *Negotiations* (pp. 177–182). New York: Columbia University Press. (Original work published 1990).

Deleuze, G., & Guattari, F. (1996). *What is philosophy?* New York: Columbia University Press. (Original work published 1991).

Deleuze, G., & Guattari, F. (2005). *A thousand plateaus: Capitalism and schizophrenia.* Minneapolis: University of Minnesota Press. (Original work published 1980).

Education Department of Western Australia. (2010). *School online.* Retrieved July 18, 2010, from http://www2.eddept.wa.edu.au/schoolprofile.

Foucault, M. (1991). *Discipline and punish: The birth of the prison.* London: Penguin Books. (Original work published 1975).

Hey, V. (2002). Horizontal solidarities and molten capitalism: The subject, intersubjectivity, self and other in late modernity. *Discourse: Studies in the Cultural Politics of Education, 23,* 227–241.

Hunter, I. (1994). *Rethinking the school: Subjectivity, bureaucracy, criticism.* St Leonards: Allen and Unwin.

Massumi, B. (2010). What concepts do: Preface to the Chinese translation of a thousand plateaus. *Deleuze Studies, 4*(1), 1–15.

McLeod, J., & Yates, L. (2006). *Making modern lives: subjectivity, schooling and social change.* Albany, NY: State University of New York Press.

O'Sullivan, S. (2006). Pragmatics for the production of subjectivity: Time for probe-heads. *Journal for Cultural Research, 10,* 309–323.

Popkewitz, T. (1998). *Struggling for the soul: The politics of schooling and the construction of the teacher.* New York: Teachers College Press.

Reid, A. (2009). Is this a revolution? A critical analysis of the Rudd government's national education agenda *Curriculum Perspectives, 29*(3), 1–13.

Semestky, I. (2008). (Pre)facing Deleuze. In I. Semetsky (Ed.), *Nomadic education: Variations on a theme by Deleuze and Guattari* (pp. vii–xxi). Rotterdam: Sense.

Semetsky, I., & Lovat, T. (2008). Knowledge in action: Towards a Deleuze–Habermasian critique in/for education. In I. Semetsky (Ed.), *Nomadic education: Variations on a theme by Deleuze and Guattari* (pp. 171–182). Rotterdam: Sense.

Smyth, J., Angus, L., Down, B., & McInerney, P. (2008). *Critically engaged learning: Connecting to young lives.* New York: Peter Lang.

Smyth, J., Down, B., & McInerney, P. (2010). *'Hanging in with kids' in tough times.* New York: Peter Lang.

Symes, C., & Preston, N. (1997). *Schools and classrooms: A cultural studies analysis of education.* South Melbourne: Longman.

Thompson, G. (2010). Acting, accidents and performativity: Challenging the hegemonic good student in secondary schools. *British Journal of Sociology of Education, 31,* 413–430.

Wetherall, M. (2009). Introduction: Negotiating liveable lives—Identity in contemporary Britain. In M. Wetherell (Ed.), *Identity in the 21st century: New trends in changing times* (pp. 1–20). New York: Palgrave MacMillan.

Identifying a K-10 Developmental Framework for Teaching Philosophy

Janette Poulton

Assessment Research Centre, University of Melbourne

Abstract

The intention of the study was to identify predictable opportunities for teachers to scaffold middle year students' philosophical learning. Such opportunities were identified in terms of students' readiness to learn certain behaviours in the context of a 'community of inquiry'. Thus it was hoped that the project would provide a useful resource for the teaching of philosophy to middle year students by ascertaining how amenable philosophical learning was to this approach. The study investigated the following questions: (i) what are the indicators of the development under the influence of the COI?; (ii) do these indicators cluster in any particular way? and (iii) is it possible to identify any clustering of indicators that suggests developmental bands?

Introduction

Philosophy programmes had been delivered in primary classrooms in Victoria, Australia, since the introduction of Lipman's Philosophy for Children (P4C) programme in 1983. In 2001 a philosophy subject was offered in the final years of secondary education and, as a flow-on, there had been efforts to introduce philosophy into lower secondary classrooms. When I began my doctoral study, there were few guidelines available for assessing this subject area during the middle years. In 2010 philosophy was being considered as a subject for the Australian National Curriculum, with the support of the Australasian Association of Philosophers, which provoked a renewed interest from academia in the development of a Kindergarten to Year 12 philosophy curriculum framework and assessment processes.

For my studies, I reviewed a period of 30 years of international research into the assessment practices of the Philosophy in Schools programme. Some attempts had been made to hypothesize or conceptualize different levels of attainment, particularly for the purpose of reporting and evaluating teachers' work. These were outcome based, but norm referenced. The criteria were varied, and the instruments were not yet standardized or shaped to reflect the specific needs of middle years students.

Howard Gardner claimed that

> ... it should prove possible to identify disparate levels of expertise in the development of an intelligence, ranging from universal beginnings through which every novice passes, to exceedingly high levels of competence. ... There may well be critical periods in the developmental history, as well as identifiable milestones, linked either to training or to physical maturation. Identification of the developmental history of the intelligence, and analysis of its susceptibility to modification and training, is of the highest importance to educational practitioners. (Gardner, 1983/1993, pp. 64–65)

My study[1] aimed to produce a developmental framework that would encourage the implementation of targeted teaching and learning programmes to support the philosophical development of middle years students.

Method

I asked:

- How do students develop in philosophical thinking in a community of inquiry (COI) context?
- Is it possible to identify any clustering of indicators that suggests developmental strands?
- To what extent is it possible to link learning to assessment within a framework of developmental philosophical thinking?

These questions were investigated through analysis of student dialogue in the context of a number of middle years philosophy classrooms in four Victorian schools. The collection of raw data in a natural classroom setting provided a critique of the 'espoused theories' that had appeared in the P4C literature. A panel of international subject matter experts assisted as judges in the selection of Indicators, the identification of strands and their organization as an instrument of assessment.

Bearing in mind Burbules' evocative metaphor '... a human statement is less like a precise laser beam of reference, and more like a knitted catch ball...' (1993, p. 11), a schema, derived from the work of discourse analysts, was developed for interpreting student utterances, consisting of strands of like skills set against bands which would indicate development in each of those strands.

The methodology for creating standards-referenced frameworks for literacy and numeracy, developed at the Assessment Research Centre at the University of Melbourne, proved useful in refining this approach. The protocols devised by Griffin and Gillis (2001) advised collection of reliable behavioural data (internally related to learning processes), identification of these data in standard form (indicators), and the organization of these indicators into both categories of like skills (strands) and clustered levels of complexity (bands) via Rasch item person modelling and/or expert subject matter panelling. A further protocol was to summarize all of the above by identifying a trait that would aptly describe the overarching dimension of learning under scrutiny; the dimension that was identified was 'Readiness to engage in a philosophical dialogue'.

The new model that emerged was an open framework that allowed for the emergence of new dimensions as further data were collected, analysed and integrated into the system. This study examined not only the behaviours of students, but also the educational perceptions of both newly trained and experienced teachers, as well as subject matter experts, to identify the actual trajectory of development towards a COI.

Findings

The study demonstrated an upward development curve consistent with ageing between the age of 8 and 14. It was noted that from ages 9 to 12 students displayed a readiness for participation in a COI, indicated by a consolidation of the basic levels of achievement. Once the basic levels had consolidated, by age 12, development seemed to occur at a faster rate, with students progressing through the next two levels of development over two years, at which point development tended to plateau. This was consistent with earlier reports that had identified large-scale developmental patterns within a COI context. It is thus hypothesized that in the earlier phase of middle years schooling, coinciding with the current transition from primary to secondary school, students should be given time to consolidate the basic patterns of behaviour identified herein.

This limited study indicated that middle years students had no preference for any particular branch of philosophy. The themes selected by students were conventionally located in the sub-branches metaphysics, ethics, ontology, logic and epistemology. This challenged the commonly held belief that teenagers were most likely to show an interest in ethical issues. Yet it was possible on the basis of the data to construct five strands, consistent with the generic P4C learning outcomes of Critical, Creative and Caring thinking, and it was clear that for middle years students those strands that were conventionally grouped in the Caring category were significant. This could be either a distinguishing feature of middle years development or a feature of all novice philosophical communities. Intellectual skills of problematizing and argument were not apparent until the lower levels of the strands identified as Self, Other and Group (personal, interpersonal and group skills) had been established. This was consistent with the views of Vygotsky (1962) and Dewey (1910/1968), who both maintained that it was an *awareness* of a common problem that led to a confrontation of ideas and to the start of the reflexive process. The developmental bands therefore began with empathy or the ability to recognize alternative points of view.

There is a commonplace idea that a sufficient mark of philosophical development is having the confidence to express a point of view and that confidence is gained by knowing about the subject matter. Recognizing that a certain competence in communication is necessary, this study challenged this simplistic view. The specific content of student beliefs was not found to be indicative of philosophical development, no matter how sophisticated such beliefs might appear to be. Students' *strategies* for forming their beliefs were treated as indicative of levels of philosophical maturity. This involved the ability to form a complex point of view, to bear in mind multiple perspectives and theoretical positions, and to evaluate that point of view according to objective criteria. There was no indication of stages in the development of the so-called critical thinking skills. The strategies used were similar to those used in dialogue and vernacular conversation.

This study indicates that a certain level of verbal and social development is prerequisite to participation in a COI, both from the point of view of unready students destabilizing the group and with the intention of successfully initiating each student into the COI. The study showed that anecdotal and monological exchanges preceded dialogical exchanges. The end of philosophical practice was observed to be achieving a state of intentional open-mindedness, referred to as 'negative capability'. The capacity 'to tolerate ambiguity and paradox, to engage in a non-defensive way with change, without being overwhelmed' (Splitter & Sharp, 1995, pp. 9–10) was observed on occasion, although not consolidated during this period of development. A COI does not simply create opportunities for the internalization of thinking skills modelled by peers, as Vygotsky (1962, p. 148) had claimed, so much as a disposition to be fair in considering alternative positions; that is, it is the development of a civil and ethical disposition.

Conclusion

The methodology inspired by the Assessment Research Centre at the University of Melbourne produced a standards-referenced framework of bands and strands that will prove of importance to educational practitioners. It provides indicators that middle year students develop certain bands of philosophical thinking in a COI context that are more to do with developing the skills of dialogue than with mastery of external critical thinking rules and knowledge.

P4C practitioners claimed that participation in the COI context could overcome student feelings of detachment, fragmentation and alienation, for example, by developing philosophical dispositions. There are clearly conceptual connections between these difficult states and the development of 'intellectual courage, humility, tolerance, integrity, perseverance and fair mindedness, respect for other persons and their points of view, and care for the procedures of inquiry' (Splitter & Sharp, 1995, pp. 9–10). These claims gain credibility in the light of this study and could be investigated using long-term studies. Our proposal is that many of these negative dispositions are best seen as *opportunities* rather than *obstacles* to learning to be fair and show respect for persons.

Note

1. I have included this summary of empirical research to contrast the recommended structure with that of Stephan Millett and Alan Tapper in this issue. Both emphasize the centrality of ethics as part of the assessment.

References

Burbules, N. (1993). *Dialogue in teaching: Theory and practice*. New York: Teachers College Press.

Dewey, J. (1968). *How we think. A restatement of the relation of reflective thinking to the educative process*. Boston, MA: Houghton Mifflin. (Original work published 1910; rev. ed. 1933).

Gardner, H. (1993). *Frames of mind: The theory of multiple intelligences*. New York: Basic Books. (Original work published 1983).

Griffin, P., & Gillis, S. (2001). A multi-source measurement approach to assessment of higher order competencies. Paper presented at the British Education Research Association Annual Conference, Cardiff University, September 7–10, 2000.

Splitter, L., & Sharp, A. (1995). *Teaching for better thinking*. Australia: Acer.

Vygotsky, L. (1962). *Thought and language*. Cambridge, MA: MIT Press.

Developing Democratic Dispositions and Enabling Crap Detection: Claims for classroom philosophy with special reference to Western Australia and New Zealand

LEON BENADE

School of Critical Studies in Education, University of Auckland

Abstract

The prominence given in national or state-wide curriculum policy to thinking, the development of democratic dispositions and preparation for the 'good life', usually articulated in terms of lifelong learning and fulfilment of personal life goals, gives rise to the current spate of interest in the role that could be played by philosophy in schools. Theorists and practitioners working in the area of philosophy for schools advocate the inclusion of philosophy in school curricula to meet these policy objectives. This article tests claims that philosophy can aid in the acquisition of democratic dispositions and develop critical thinking and considers to the extent to which these aims are compatible with each other. These considerations are located in the context of certain policy statements relating to the curricula of Western Australia and New Zealand.

Introduction

While the official status of philosophy teaching in the primary and junior secondary phase of schools internationally is yet to be well established, there is international evidence of officially sanctioned philosophy in the senior secondary phase (Hand & Winstanley, 2008a, pp. xi–xii). It is in this regard that this article considers curriculum documentation used in schools in New Zealand and Western Australia. Despite the

Leon Benade is currently at School of Education, Auckland University of Technology.

lack of evidence of the 'official' inclusion of philosophy in the primary and junior secondary phases, an approach that has become well established in many schools is Philosophy for Children (P4C) and its associated teaching methodology, the community of enquiry (COPE)[1] (Hand & Winstanley, 2008a). Developed in the 1970s by Matthew Lipman, then professor at Montclair State University, New Jersey, P4C initially had primary students in mind. The COPE is, however, a methodology that can be and is employed with secondary age students in the subject philosophy in general (McCall, 2009), and this article will therefore not concern itself specifically with P4C.

Further enquiries in this area are timely because of the interest shown by state and national curricula in thinking and the development of democratic dispositions as evidenced in relevant policy documentation about to be considered. The starting point of this article is a set of claims made by proponents of classroom philosophy in *Philosophy in schools* (Hand & Winstanley, 2008b), a collection that reflects on many key debates about classroom philosophy. This article uses the policy statements reviewed below as a context, it introduces the set of claims made on behalf of classroom philosophy, and it considers the COPE and specific exemplar classroom philosophy curriculum statements from New Zealand and Western Australia in regard to these promises made on behalf of philosophy in schools.

Policy Statements

Justifications for including philosophy in schools usually point to its ability to encourage enquiry and critical thinking and develop the dispositions of reasonableness, tolerance and patience, and skills of communication and cooperative participation (Splitter, 1995; Splitter & Sharp, 1995). The currently high levels of interest in academic literature in the role and place of philosophy in school are partly driven by state and national curricular emphases on the development of these attributes in students. A consideration of certain curriculum policy documents chosen from Western Australia and New Zealand will provide a sense of the 'official' view on the importance or otherwise of democratic behaviours and dispositions on one hand, and critical thinking on the other, reflected by these two authorities.

Western Australia

The Curriculum Framework of Western Australia sets out seven specific principles that include five clusters of 'core values', two of which are related to democratic behaviours and dispositions appropriate to the maintenance of democracy and democratic institutions. The value clusters are further detailed on the inside cover of the Framework document. The overarching statement is quoted here:

Principles of the Curriculum Framework

The Curriculum Framework for Western Australian schools is underpinned by seven key principles. These principles guide schools in whole-school planning and curriculum development ... [These principles include] an explicit acknowledgment of core values [including]:

- *respect and concern for others and their rights*, resulting in sensitivity to and concern for the well-being of others, respect for others and a search for constructive ways of managing conflict;
- *social and civic responsibility*, resulting in a commitment to exploring and promoting the common good; meeting individual needs in ways which do not infringe the rights of others; participating in democratic processes; social justice and cultural diversity. (Curriculum Council of Western Australia, 1998, p. 16)

New Zealand

In contrast, directives that could be related to the development of democratic behaviours and dispositions in the New Zealand Curriculum are much more abbreviated and somewhat scattered in their overarching statements. Nevertheless, here are some relevant points from overarching statements of 'principles' and 'values':

Principles: Foundations of curriculum decision making. The principles ... should underpin all school decision making ... [These include]

- *Future focus*: The curriculum encourages students to ... explor[e] such significant future-focused issues as ... citizenship ...

Values: To be encouraged, modelled and explored. ... by holding these values and acting on them ... we are able to live together and thrive ... [The values include]

- *Equity* through fairness and social justice;
- *Community and participation* for the common good;
- *Respect* themselves, others, and human rights. (Ministry of Education, 2007, pp. 9–10)

In both cases, *respect* features, particularly in relation to the rights of others. Both also emphasize *participation*, in communities and democratic processes. A third feature is a range of ideas that could be loosely grouped under the title of *social responsibility*, which includes concerns about social justice, equity and diversity.

The Western Australian document is far more promising as it analyses each of the core values. This allows teachers in that jurisdiction to plan programmes and outcomes that could show progression within each of the supplied descriptors. In contrast, New Zealand teachers are left somewhat in the dark, the only descriptions literally being what is quoted above. It may be questioned, however, whether the more open language of the New Zealand Curriculum in fact ensures what Gregory (1997) alludes to, namely the space for students to work out the content of these dispositions for themselves. Regardless of the answer, what is clear for teachers in both jurisdictions is that they must devise programmes that will develop these dispositions of *respect, participation* and *social responsibility*.

A further interest, as previously noted, leading to an intensification of interest in the topic of philosophy in schools in current international scholarship is driven in part by the call made in official national and state curricula for schools to develop 'thinking' skills. Further examples can be drawn from Western Australia and New Zealand.
Western Australia:

> This section of the Overarching Statement describes the outcomes which all students need to attain in order to become lifelong learners, achieve their potential in their personal and working lives and play an active part in civic and economic life ...

> [Outcome] 6: Students visualize consequences, think laterally, recognize opportunity and potential and are prepared to test options.

> In approaching issues and problems, students think laterally, offer possibilities, explore and evaluate new ideas, and generate a range of positions and solutions. (Curriculum Council of Western Australia, 1998, pp. 20, 23)

New Zealand:

> The New Zealand Curriculum identifies five key competencies ... People use these competencies to live, learn, work, and contribute as active members of their communities ... [They include]

> *Thinking*

> Thinking is about using creative, critical, and metacognitive processes to make sense of information, experiences, and ideas. (Ministry of Education, 2007, p. 12)

The crucial phrase 'critical thinking' is largely absent; indeed, searches of both documents reflect scant use of the terms 'critical thinking' or 'thinking critically'. Both extracts above regard thinking as a 'competency' or an 'outcome' that is instrumental to living 'the good life', which is defined in terms of economic and civic responsibilities, in addition to the attainment of personal life goals. Neither statement makes reference to reasoning; the New Zealand statement treats 'critical thinking' as one kind of thinking amongst others; the Western Australian statement defines thinking as 'lateral thinking' which could be related to the New Zealand use of 'creative thinking'; both statements attempt to list processes that may engage a person when thinking, either at a general level (New Zealand) or more specifically (Western Australia). Both statements use references associated with cognitive psychology, valued highly in contemporary education. I assume the philosophical position that 'thinking', and in particular, 'critical thinking', is a normative and ethical matter, not a matter of competent mastery of discrete processes. Being a 'critical thinker', it will be suggested in this article, is a disposition, or 'critical spirit' (Bailin & Siegel, 2002; Daniel & Auriac, 2011) which allows one to detect faulty reasoning and provide reasons for rejecting it. The question of interest to this article is whether the use of philosophy in schools will develop this disposition in students.

The policy references above do not provide detailed rationales or guidance to teachers and schools; however they are representative of curriculum policy documents of the early twenty-first century. Detailed application of these broad policy directives in both jurisdictions will be considered later. The discussion now turns to consider the claims made on behalf of philosophy in schools in respect to the achievement of democratic dispositions and critical thinking.

Claims Made for Philosophy in Schools

Claims No. 1 and 2

> Citizens of a democratic state are required to think and deliberate impartially on a range of contentious moral issues; the traditional forms of moral and religious thinking are poor preparation for this task; philosophical education in schools that considers controversial issues will better equip tomorrow's voter to make responsible democratic decisions. (Brighouse, 2008, pp. 61–62)

> P4C's democratic and egalitarian community of enquiry pedagogy allows pupils to ask questions .... (Murris, 2008, pp. 105, 106, 107)

Claim No. 3

> The argument is that philosophy is a powerful subject and that philosophising, or philosophic enquiry, is the optimum pedagogy for fostering the essential skills and dispositions of critical thinking. (Winstanley, 2008, p. 85)

The claims therefore are first that philosophy in schools develops the capacity for morally responsible democratic decision making; secondly that the COPE has the attributes of being democratic and egalitarian, and thus, by implication, participation in this community will develop these attributes in participants; and thirdly, that teaching philosophy in schools will develop critical thinking. The first two are grouped together as they are claims regarding the ability of philosophy in schools and the COPE methodology to develop democratic dispositions; the third concerns critical thinking, which, it is argued, will emanate from general philosophical programmes.

Because these claims are made on behalf of philosophy in schools generally, and the COPE methodology specifically, it is important to clarify that this article is less interested in an explicit consideration of Lipman's P4C being rather more focused on the general concept of including philosophy in school, and in particular the COPE as an approach, which can be used beyond P4C. A brief summation of the COPE methodology and an outline of the philosophy curriculum statements of Western Australia and New Zealand precede a consideration of these claims. The development of morally democratic citizenship, democratic dispositions and egalitarianism will be contextualized by reference to the curriculum policy statements reviewed earlier, to ascertain what, if any, guidance may exist for teachers in these policy statements. This will be followed by an assessment of the potential of the exemplar classroom curriculum programmes and the COPE method to meet these policy requirements. Critical thinking will be characterized, and the possibilities presented by the exemplar philosophy curriculum statements to develop such thinking will be considered.

The Community of Philosophical Enquiry

The notion of the COPE has both the physical quality of a material reality and a deeper, more profound existence in the hearts and minds of its participants (Splitter & Sharp, 1995; Cassidy, 2007). What might this look, sound and feel like? Essentially, a circular formation of perhaps no more than 20 participants, with some suggesting 15 to be optimal (McCall, 2009, p. 132). Larger classes could be subdivided into smaller units. Status is irrelevant, and each participant (including the teacher, if seated) is arranged so that no-one appears to be 'in authority'; each participant is able to have eye contact with everyone else in the group.

The facilitator (usually the teacher) may guide the community through a text or a series of exercises. Participants are called upon to generate questions that arise from the text. These are likely to range from the procedural and factual to the psychological and the philosophical. It is, of course, the latter which are desired. Nevertheless, each question is valued; each questioner validated. The public sharing of questions is one method whereby questioning skills are honed. The community has an agreed set of ground rules that govern the ebb and flow of discussion (such as speaking only when in possession of the 'talking stick' or another appropriate object). Respect for others is a consistent focus for the facilitator and participants. The facilitator may prompt further questions, or may merely silently record whatever is said.

The group is trained so that individuals ask their peers for clarification, request examples, and critique, in a mutually supportive way, their additional questions and truth claims. The COPE therefore has a particular self-correcting quality. The ongoing discussion is not conversation, as it requires cognitive effort and a search for meaning (Daniel & Auriac, 2011). Moreover, it makes demands on participants to present their views logically and to engage in logical analysis (McCall, 2009). Self-correction is deepened by the group summation at the end of an enquiry and the reflection of its members on the quality of discussion (Fisher, 2003). The sense of 'community' develops over time as participants feel supported, affirmed and able to 'take risks'. Well-being grows from increasing self-esteem, thinking becomes sharper and critical faculties are honed in the mutual quest to satisfy the curiosity of participants (Splitter & Sharp, 1995; Cassidy, 2007).

Two Exemplar Philosophy Curriculum Statements: Western Australia and New Zealand

Western Australia

The senior secondary course in Philosophy and Ethics was introduced in 2008. Students are taught the specific skills of enquiry, reasoning and judgement, and the

Rationale statement that introduces the course notes that 'Philosophy and Ethics aims to empower students to make independent judgements on the basis of reason' (Curriculum Council of Western Australia., 2010, p. 3).

Course content passes through Stages 1–3, of which Stages 2 and 3 are assessed by public examination. The preferred teaching methodology is the COPE, favoured for its potential to develop critical reasoning. Course content is arranged so as to cover issues of increasing complexity across epistemology (how do we know?), metaphysics (what is real?) and ethics (how should we live?). Access to course design, syllabus, assessment and support material, and past examinations is available at the Curriculum Council website.[2] The course design provides a clear, if systematic, scope and sequence for two units of each of the three stages across the content areas mentioned. Examples of course content include:

- distinguishing between strong and weak arguments (Stage 2)
- the conceptual difficulties of free-will, determinism and agency (Stage 2)
- government interference and surveillance (Stage 2)
- moral virtues and friendship (Stage 1) (Curriculum Council of Western Australia, 2010, pp. 12-16.).

New Zealand

Buried deeply in the senior secondary curriculum guides for social sciences, within the official Ministry of Education website, *Te Kete Ipurangi*, is a newly added guide called 'Philosophy', which 'is about acquiring wisdom through free inquiry. It explores fundamental questions about the world and our place in it, such as:

- What is real?
- How should I live, and who should decide?' (Ministry of Education, 2009).

The Rationale statement lists 'Think critically' as a reason to study philosophy, noting that the 'reasoned exchange of ideas in the classroom fosters tolerance of and respect for others' (Ministry of Education, 2009).

Course content passes through three learning levels (6–8), aimed at Years 11–13. There are no uniquely designed assessments for philosophy. Instead, a range of internal achievement and unit standards are cross-referenced from various other learning areas on the New Zealand Qualifications Framework, including Social Studies, Art History, Religion, English, History, Science and Classical Studies. There is no direct suggestion for a preferred teaching methodology, although 'methods of inquiry' are suggested to include clarification, exploration and evaluation. Content is framed in terms of learning outcomes that are divided into four strands: inquiry, reasoning, philosophical perspectives and applied philosophy. Progression statements for each strand are provided at each level. Indicators include:

- justify positions on philosophical ideas (Level 6)
- illustrate ideas from various philosophical perspectives (Level 6)

- develop and evaluate reasoned arguments (Level 7)
- judge viability of basic assumptions in issues (Level 7)
- connect philosophical ideas and critique them (Level 8).

Can Classroom Philosophy Programmes and the Community of Philosophic Enquiry Develop Democratic Dispositions?

The first of the claims to developing democratic dispositions was in reference to the development of the capacity for morally responsible democratic decision making; and the second referred specifically to the COPE, which is said to have the attributes of being democratic and egalitarian, and thus, by implication, capable of developing these attributes in participants. In fact, it is very difficult to separate programmes of classroom philosophy and the COPE methodology. As noted, the Western Australia exemplar of classroom philosophy makes the COPE method central to its programme (Curriculum Council of Western Australia, 2010), whereas the New Zealand exemplar programme does not direct teachers to a specific pedagogical approach. The following discussion will proceed by contextualizing a consideration of the claim that classroom philosophy and the COPE will encourage the development of democratic dispositions against the framework of the policy documentation quoted earlier.

The earlier analysis of the principles and values of both the Western Australia and New Zealand Curriculum highlighted the democratic dispositions of *respect, participation* and *social responsibility*. Teachers in both jurisdictions are required to devise programmes and pedagogical approaches to develop these dispositions.

Respect

The COPE depends largely for its success on the agreement of the whole group on the ground rules governing enquiry and debate. These procedures will come to be regarded as having both intrinsic and procedural value, and will ultimately be recognized as a source of dispositional training (Gregory, 1997).

Respect demands a validation of the other, which occurs when the facilitator acknowledges each person's questions and contributions. This validation amounts to a legitimation of each person's contribution and aids in the social construction of knowledge provided that validation is *critical* and not mere patronization. Respect encourages impartiality, as all views are taken into account and judged by their merits, and in light of the arguments put forward in their favour, even in the matter of formulating procedural rules.

The concept of respect is thus central to the procedures of a COPE. Do the course offerings of the two jurisdictions provide the content for developing respect? The New Zealand curriculum statement on philosophy makes a single reference to 'respect', in its rationale for teaching/studying philosophy at school: 'The reasoned exchange of ideas in the classroom fosters tolerance of and respect for others' (Ministry of Education, 2009, p. 1). The reference to 'reasoned exchange of ideas' is noteworthy as it may echo a COPE context. The content of the curriculum statement is, however, not very helpful or directive in its suggestions for objectives or contexts that may explicitly focus on the development of respect. Aspects of the intended outcomes and learning contexts of these strands may have the development of respect as an outcome, although on the evidence, this may be unintended.

The Curriculum Council of Western Australia syllabus for Philosophy and Ethics details four outcomes for its three-year senior secondary programme, the first of which is 'Philosophical and ethical inquiry', whose intention is that students 'use investigative methods to think and argue philosophically' (2010, p. 4) using a COPE methodology. Course content is divided between epistemology, metaphysics and ethics, the latter concerned with 'communities and cultures' as one of its contexts, from which perspective 'respect' is studied (2010, pp. 5, 18). This statement is more rigorous than its New Zealand counterpart, by its directive outline of learning contexts that could develop an understanding of respect, and its insistence on the COPE as a mechanism for teaching respect.

Participation

Participation in a COPE depends on students internalizing the merits of self-discipline and turn taking, so that every person who wishes to contribute may do so. Individuals will feel secure enough to make contributions, even if they are offbeat or marginal to the topic, when the conditions that encourage respect exist, including a safe learning environment created by the teacher (Splitter & Sharp, 1995, p. 20). The challenge for the teacher/facilitator is to draw out contributions from those less willing, which is considerably more challenging when using the COPE in a secondary setting (McCall, 2009, pp. 155–157).

It is a question for those who may be critical of classroom philosophy and the COPE whether these are merely opportunities for talk, with no obligation to take action. The New Zealand philosophy curriculum statement makes no mention at all of 'participation', although one may expect that its 'applied philosophy' strand holds some promise. However, the indicators take students from recognizing implications and assumptions to judging their viability and ultimately evaluating their viability (Ministry of Education, 2009, pp. 7, 11, 14), though it is unclear what the difference may be between 'judging' and 'evaluating'. It appears that the New Zealand programme for secondary students invests its hope for participation in keen teachers and students, but not in the text of its course description. Is the Western Australia example any better?

While the term 'participation' appears frequently in the Philosophy and Ethics syllabus, it does so only in relation to participation in the COPE. The term 'action' is more helpful, although its appearance in learning contexts appears to be confined to a consideration of the implications of human and personal action, in relation to the outcome already referred to, namely 'Philosophical and ethical inquiry'. However, there is a further, more hopeful outcome, which requires students to: 'Apply[ ] and relat[e] philosophical and ethical understandings, [by] … reflect[ing] on, evaluat[ing] and respond[ing] to a range of human issues by selecting from a repertoire of philosophical and ethical strategies' (Curriculum Council of Western Australia, 2010, p. 4). Here at least, if even only in theory, is the possibility of developing a participative approach to democracy.

Social Responsibility

The social responsibility mentioned in the policy statements would include the promotion of social justice, equity and diversity. Social justice is promoted by a COPE whenever individuals on the fringes, whose voices are rarely heard, are encouraged by their peers to become involved.

The great democratic virtue of tolerance is to diversity what impartiality is to equity. By listening patiently and carefully to the wide range of differing views, and having one's own views subject to scrutiny by others who may decide to reject them, one develops the tolerance required of living in a pluralistic society. Likewise, weighing up options, giving each person a fair hearing and being prepared to self-correct and retreat from a position is a recognition that each member of the COPE is capable of reasoning, and that each person is fallible (Cassidy, 2007, p. 124).

The contribution of philosophy to the development of tolerance is put forward by the New Zealand curriculum statement as a rationale for its inclusion in the curriculum. Each of its four strands (inquiry, reasoning, philosophical perspectives and applied philosophy) provide scope for this development. Its scant detail and failure to encourage any form of action, however, lead to the conclusion that 'social justice' may be, at best, an academic concept in this course.

In its rationale for the study of philosophy and ethics, the Western Australia exemplar notes that the course contributes to students' understanding of being 'a citizen who recognises the rights of others and makes choices in the social, civic and environmental spheres' (Curriculum Council of Western Australia, 2010, p. 3). Its explanation of the metaphysics and ethics course components provides evidence of wide-ranging questions that consider conceptions of ultimate reality; persons; governance; communities and cultures; self and others (2010, p. 5). Suggested topics that follow, while not detailed, are located in a thoroughly conceptualized programme of work, giving teachers much stimulus for presenting a relevant and vibrant course that may indeed deliver on the promise of developing a sense of social justice in students.

Is the Community of Philosophic Enquiry Democratic and Egalitarian?

The COPE, which has enquiry as its focus, may also, coincidentally, have democracy as its focus, because the procedures underpinning both are similar (Gregory, 1997). COPE encourages certain behaviours: rule making and following; careful listening; asking questions; choosing, selecting, deciding; turn taking; seeking, developing and adjusting answers and arguments in relation to questions; argumentation, which involves suggesting a response or position in relation to a question or statement, then giving and defending reasons for that response or position; seeking clarification or more information; challenging the responses of others and providing a counter-response; no name-calling, put-downs or personal attacks; participating and contributing; and finally, reflection on process, content or method. While these acts may resemble democratic acts (such as following certain rules, deliberating in a community and participating), this does not mean members of a COPE are necessarily likely to be democratic. Successful democracy, like successful enquiry, requires individuals who are democratically disposed.

Dispositions are personal tendencies or inclinations that guide or direct persons to act and think in certain ways. These are built up by practice, but this does not mean that they are followed in a robotically habitual way; rather, dispositions are knowing and intelligent acts of reason (Ryle, 1949). Reasonableness will be the result of practice through COPE in some of the behaviours outlined above (Splitter & Sharp, 1995, p. 6). It is hoped that these behaviours may also result in dispositions to virtuous conduct such as tolerance and patience, care and compassion, respect, self-discipline, impartiality and participation. As Ryle suggests, however, the acquisition of these dispositions over time is no guarantee that their holders will always act in predictable ways (1949, pp. 41–44). A good reason for this is that dispositions tell us *how* to think generally and not *what* to think in regard to certain situations.

One of the crucial weaknesses of the COPE methodology is that its deliberations are not *required* to lead to action (Cevallos-Estarellas & Sigurdardottir, 2000). Democratic notions emphasizing majority participation conflict with liberal notions (with which democracy is frequently allied) that emphasize the rights of the individual (Cevallos-Estarellas & Sigurdardottir). The COPE puts no pressure at all on the individual student or group of students to turn their ideas to action. In this sense, philosophy in school, using a COPE, is reduced to no more than an intellectual exercise aimed at heightened cognitive rationality for the individual. However, the COPE methodology is aimed at creating dispositions that will lead to actions consistent with democratic principles.

Murris claimed that the COPE models an egalitarian community (2008, p. 107). The generally optimistic tenor of COPE proponents (e.g. Splitter & Sharp, 1995; Cleghorn, 2002; Fisher, 2003; Cassidy, 2007; Hand & Winstanley, 2008b; Murris, 2008; McCall, 2009; Winstanley, 2008) does not readily admit the power exercised by students who display oppositional behaviour patterns (Burgh & Yorshansky, 2011). Such students may effectively derail the COPE by defiance, rule breaking or sullenness. Murris notes that secondary students 'are often suspicious' and find 'sitting in a circle an alien experience' (Murris, 2008, p. 114). The 'egalitarian' nature of the COPE may be further called into question as power must still lie in the hands of the teacher. Much depends on the goodwill of the teacher to give the COPE the room to explore and enquire, thus potentially controlling the development of democratic dispositions. It is the teacher who has to release power (Murris, 2008).

The potential of the COPE to develop democratic dispositions is nevertheless significant, if one abandons 'thin' or 'minimal' notions of democracy that focus on elitist representation of a passive majority through the electoral system (Cevallos-Estarellas & Sigurdardottir, 2000; Enslin & White, 2002) or trained individual behaviour rather than a disposition to act autonomously in the interests of the community. These writers note the value of thinking about democracy as a deliberative act that requires greater communal participation by citizens. This notion of a 'strong' democracy is deepened by schools that engage their students in *democratic education* rather than *education for democracy*. Exercises in citizenship or civics (such as the call in the New Zealand Curriculum for a focus on citizenship) are preparation for a 'thin' democracy; the COPE has the potential, provided it develops a service, outreach or action component, to encourage democratic dispositions among its members.

Critical Thinking and Crap Detection

The discussion that follows is premised on the position that *critical thinking* is a desirable educational aim in modern schooling because a disposition to critical thinking is the mark of a rational and autonomous person. That such a person can think critically will serve that person well in all aspects of life, so on that basis, adhering to this premise allows one to occupy the same room as those who claim 'thinking' for instrumental 'lifelong' purposes.

A simple statement of critical thinking was made four decades ago when Postman and Weingartner, reflecting on an Ernest Hemingway comment, referred to an '… education that would set out to cultivate … experts at "crap detecting"' (1969, p. 16). They went on to suggest that this meant schools should 'cultivate the anthropological perspective' (p. 17). What they had in mind was a person adept at both living in the world and being able to step back from it and to signal warning bells at signs of decay. Such a person is an active *agent* in the process of meaning making. The point is illustrated by Freire when he speaks of the subject being not *in* the world as an animal may be, but *with* the world; not *adapting* to the world, but actively seeking to *transform* the world (Freire, 1985, p. 68) through the creative power of thought and work. At first glance this seems to contradict the democratic disposition to show respect and tolerance, and to form a coherent part of a changing society.

'Critical thinking' has elements of creativity, impartiality, reflectivity and fortitude. The disposition to critical thinking will mean that the individual takes nothing for granted and constantly questions and enquires. This 'crap detection' is discomforting and not always conventional, hence the virtue of courage. For Bailin and Siegel (2002), this disposition is defined by (1) the value of good reasoning to critical thinkers, (2) their search for reasons and assessment of those reasons, and (3) the willingness to be guided by this process.

The preceding remarks have raised questions about taxonomies, associated with the vast range of commercially available 'silver bullet solutions' that 'tend to focus on improving cognitive processes … rather than forming the habit of acting and believing in accordance with reasons' (Winstanley, 2008, p. 90). An example is the SOLO taxonomy,[3] currently used in several New Zealand schools, which focuses on a description of particular stages at which a student's thinking may be functioning without reference to the quality of thought. A student could be working at the 'extended abstract' level, yet not be thinking critically at all. In ignoring the capacity to detect crap, the SOLO taxonomy does not distinguish between training and education, between obedience to and mastery of certain rules and the ability to use those rules pragmatically.

The definitive comments above about 'critical thinking' grouped together several items that get a separate billing in the curriculum policies quoted at the start of this article. Those policies enumerate creativity, reflection and critical thinking as separate 'kinds' of thinking. It is this approach which underpins taxonomies and which fails to recognize, first, that the other 'types' of thinking are actually contexts for critical thinking (Bailin & Siegel, 2002), and secondly, that one could be engaged in reflective or creative thought without being critical, just as suggested with abstract thinking. Lipman has commented that self-reflective thinking (the metacognition to which the New Zealand Curriculum makes frequent reference) or 'thinking about thinking' is not critical unless it is used in community and in reference to the thinking of others. Until that happens, it is merely 'thinking about thinking' (Lipman, 1988).

What then is the contribution that the two exemplar philosophy curriculum statements can make to the development of critical thinking? The Western Australian course has signs of rigour and development that allow philosophy to exist as a stand-alone subject in its own right, which has some concern with the canon of philosophy. The New Zealand example has a much looser structure, resembling an evolved model of P4C, by focusing on ideas and argumentation. The absence of a unique assessment programme weakens its credibility, although the integration of course content into assessments drawn from other learning areas is an advantage. This summation draws together two of the key debates in the literature concerning philosophy as a stand-alone or an integrated subject and teaching the canon or *doing philosophy* (e.g. Hand & Winstanley, 2008b).

Both courses have a commitment to the development of critical thinking, and allow for course content that will provide the scope for such development. However, the rigidity of the scope and sequence of Western Australia and the specification of learning outcomes of New Zealand could limit the development of such thinking. The choice of COPE by the former (and potentially by the latter) keeps alive the possibility of the mutual meta-reflective thinking Lipman believed to be a function of critical thinking or crap detection. Similarly, the meta-dialogical approach of a COPE allows active disagreement (Murris, 2008) and the 'reasoned exchange of ideas' (Ministry of Education, 2009) that are essential to critical thinking. Both courses make it clear that knowledge is contestable, and that there are no fixed or immediate answers, which stimulate the development of virtuous courage. In both cases, the attendance of students in philosophy-based courses will help to provide more training in the disposition of critical thinking than if those courses did not exist.

Conclusion

This article has acknowledged that the development of democratic dispositions and critical thinking is a typical policy requirement in many Western education settings today. Certain claims are made on behalf of classroom philosophy and a particular pedagogical approach (COPE) to meet these objectives. Using the policy settings of Western Australia and New Zealand, the value of such programmes is examined in attaining the dual policy aims of developing democratic dispositions and critical thinking.

Can courses of philosophy in schools and a pedagogical approach using the COPE develop democratic dispositions and critical thinking in students? A focus on philosophy, whether it is integrated or stand-alone, provides teachers and students the opportunity of investigating topics of critical sociopolitical, economic and personal interest that may only occur incidentally in other areas of the curriculum. Furthermore, as many of these topics require exploration and investigation rather than 'coverage' the leverage that can be exercised by critical reasoning is considerable. This point is significant as it is an acknowledgement that 'crap detection', or what Freire calls 'critical consciousness' (Freire, 1973, 1985), is the pinnacle of desirable educational aims (and considers 'creative' and 'lateral' thinking as contexts for critical thinking). Certainly, both exemplars considered here (more so the Western Australian than the New Zealand) offer the scope required to develop programmes that will challenge students.

To the extent that both programmes use the COPE or similar discursive methodologies, they also stand to develop democratic dispositions. Much will depend, however, on the teacher, and it may be suggested that the New Zealand programme would be enriched by encouraging COPE as a structure for teachers who may lack the confidence or experience required to manage open debate and discussion. The COPE does rely on, and gives participants opportunities for, engagement with many of the behaviours associated with democratic inclinations. However, both the COPE and the exemplar programmes considered stop short at encouraging a call to action, and it is in this area that more work is required, to develop a 'strong' sense of democracy that is participative.

Notes

1. The Standard English 'enquire' is favoured over the American 'inquire'. Henceforth in this article, 'community of enquiry' will be referred to as 'COPE' for 'community of philosophic enquiry'.
2. http://www.curriculum.wa.edu.au/internet/Senior_Secondary/Courses/Philosophy_and_Ethics
3. Structure of Observed Learning Outcomes, which is clearly outlined at http://www.learningandteaching.info/learning/solo.htm

References

Bailin, S., & Siegel, H. (2002). Critical thinking. In N. Blake, P. Smeyers, R. Smith & P. Standish (Eds.), *The Blackwell guide to the philosophy of education*. Blackwell Reference Online, Blackwell.

Brighouse, H. (2008). The role of philosophical thinking in teaching controversial issues. In M. Hand & C. Winstanley (Eds.), *Philosophy in schools* (pp. 61–77). London: Continuum.

Burgh, G., & Yorshansky, M. (2011). Communities of inquiry: Politics, power and group dynamics. *Educational Philosophy and Theory, 43*, 436–452.

Cassidy, C. (2007). *Thinking children*. London: Continuum.

Cevallos-Estarellas, P., & Sigurdardottir, B. (2000). The community of inquiry as a means for cultivating democracy. *Inquiry: Critical Thinking Across the Disciplines, 19*, 45–57.

Cleghorn, P. (2002). Why philosophy with children? Retrieved August 24, 2010, from http://www.aude-education.co.uk/philosophy.htm

Curriculum Council of Western Australia. (1998). The Curriculum Framework. Retrieved April 14, 2010, from http://www.curriculum.wa.edu.au/internet/Years_K10/Curriculum_Framework/Curriculum_Framework

Curriculum Council of Western Australia. (2010). Philosophy and ethics. Retrieved April 16, 2010, from http://www.curriculum.wa.edu.au/internet/Senior_Secondary/Courses/WACE_Courses/Philosophy_and_Ethics

Daniel, M.-F., & Auriac, E. (2011). Philosophy, critical thinking and Philosophy for Children. *Educational Philosophy and Theory, 43*, 415–435.

Enslin, P., & White, P. (2002). Democratic citizenship. In N. Blake, P. Smeyers, R. Smith & P. Standish (Eds.), *The Blackwell guide to the philosophy of education*. Blackwell Reference Online: Blackwell.

Fisher, R. (2003). *Teaching thinking: Philosophical enquiry in the classroom* (2nd ed). London: Continuum.

Freire, P. (1973). *Education: The practice of freedom*. London: Writers and Readers Collective.

Freire, P. (1985). *The politics of education: Culture, power and liberation*. London: Macmillan.

Gregory, M. (1997). Democracy and care in the community of inquiry. *Inquiry: Critical Thinking Across the Disciplines, 17*, 40–50.

Hand, M., & Winstanley, C. (2008a). Introduction. In M. Hand & C. Winstanley (Eds.), *Philosophy in schools* (pp. x–xviii). London: Continuum.

Hand, M., & Winstanley, C. (Eds.). (2008). *Philosophy in schools*. London: Continuum.

Lipman, M. (1988). Critical thinking—What can it be? *Educational Leadership, 46*, 38–43.

McCall, C. (2009). *Transforming thinking: Philosophical inquiry in the primary and secondary classroom*. London: Routledge.

Ministry of Education. (2007). *The New Zealand Curriculum*. Wellington: Learning Media.

Ministry of Education. (2009). Philosophy. Retrieved March 30, 2010, from http://seniorsecondary.tki.org.nz/Social-sciences/Philosophy

Murris, K. (2008). Autonomous and authentic thinking through philosophy with picture books. In M. Hand & C. Winstanley (Eds.), *Philosophy in schools* (pp. 105–118). London: Continuum.

Postman, N., & Weingartner, C. (1969). *Teaching as a subversive activity*. Harmondsworth: Penguin Books.

Ryle, G. (1949). *The concept of mind*. Harmondsworth: Penguin.

Splitter, L. (1995). On the theme of teaching for higher order thinking skills. *Inquiry: Critical Thinking Across the Disciplines, 14*, 52–65.

Splitter, L., & Sharp, A. (1995). *Teaching for better thinking: The classroom community of inquiry*. Melbourne: Australian Council for Educational Research.

Winstanley, C. (2008). Philosophy and the development of critical thinking. In M. Hand & C. Winstanley (Eds.), *Philosophy in schools* (pp. 85–95). London: Continuum.

Philosophy, Art or Pedagogy? How should children experience education?

CHRISTINE DODDINGTON

Faculty of Education, University of Cambridge

Abstract

There are various programmes currently advocated for ways in which children might encounter philosophy as an explicit part of their education. An analysis of these reveals the ways in which they are predicated on views of what constitutes philosophy. In the sense in which they are inquiry based, purport to encourage the pursuit of puzzlement and contribute towards creating democratic citizens, these programmes either implicitly rest on the work of John Dewey or explicitly use his work as the main warrant for their approach. This article explores what might count as educational in the practice of children 'doing' philosophy, by reconsidering Dewey's notion of 'experience'. The educational desire to generate inquiry, thought and democracy is not lost, but a view that philosophy takes its impetus from wonder is introduced to help re-evaluate what might count as educational experience in a Deweyan sense.

Introduction: Philosophy in Schools

According to a UK Education agency (QCA) and the National Foundation for Educational Research in the UK, a comparison of the curricular and assessment frameworks of 20 more economically developed countries shows that 'The overwhelming majority of children in Europe, North America and Australasia have no statutory or otherwise established entitlement to encounter philosophy during the period of compulsory schooling' (Hand & Winstanley, 2008, p. xi). However, a brief trawl of the internet is enough to show that there is a whole range of initiatives involving and promoting children and philosophy around the globe. It is possible to categorize them in a number of ways. First, in broad terms, there are versions that centre on engaging children in philosophizing, while other approaches are more concerned with instructing children in some of the 'great ideas of philosophers'. In the latter form, philosophical ideas and beliefs can be introduced to children under the guise of a humanities programme or through cultural or social studies. Jostein Gaarder has said that *Sophie's world* (1995) arose out of his desire to teach young adolescents a philosophy as a history of ideas. This distinction also underpins claims as to whether children can be seen as 'natural philosophers' or whether 'students lack the ability to gain anything of philosophical value' from encountering the 'canon' of philosophical thought (Benade, 2010, p. 209).

Robert Fisher suggests a dualism between formal and informal philosophy. Where 'formal' philosophy refers to the systematic, academic discipline, 'informal' philosophy is seen as the 'discursive or dialogic engagement with conceptual problems and questions of existential concern without recourse to the specialist resources of academic philosophy' (Fisher, 2008, p. 100). This article will follow the notion of 'informal' philosophy and focus on the more common practice, at least in the UK, of students actively 'doing' philosophy. It can be described as a category of 'thinking skill', embedded in courses designed to encourage critical thinking, or is part of what is presented as the general use of 'dialogue' in the classroom. My intention is to select from some of the writing of those who advocate particular views or methods for using philosophy with children and to focus more generally on discussion in the classroom. What follows is an analysis of some of the programmes in this informal philosophy.

Matthew Lipman's *Philosophy for children* (P4C) aimed to produce a Deweyan conception of a school-based community of inquiry (Lipman, 2003, pp. 81–104). The influence of Lipman's work is found in a number of programmes advocating philosophy for children. Examples found in the UK include the work of Karin Murris, who trained with Lipman, and who has been influential in the use of picture books as a stimulus for young children doing philosophy (www.dialogueworks.co.uk) and The Society for Advancing Philosophical Enquiry and Reflection (SAPERE) (www.sapere.org.uk), which aims to promote philosophical inquiry with children and communities. Psychologist Robert Fisher has researched philosophy in primary schools and has been influential in promoting children philosophizing through stories, poems and games (Fisher, 2003).

Philosophy as Discussion: Different Versions, Different Purposes

While the idea of children doing philosophy generally focuses on discussion, advocates articulate different purposes of discussion depending on their conception of philosophy. Michael Hand (Hand & Winstanley, 2008) avoids arguing that children *should* do philosophy, but claims that children are *capable* of doing philosophy, so he asks whether there is a philosophical method that is 'i) central to the mainstream practice of philosophy and ii) capable of being understood and applied by children' (Hand, 2008, p. 13). He selects a method drawn from R. S. Peters that philosophy is 'concerned with forms of thought and argument expressed in "What do you mean?" and "How do you know?"' (Hand, 2008, p. 11), believing that the subject matter of philosophy is 'the concepts, theories and presuppositions present in various disciplines and in everyday life', in contrast with a traditional focus on 'the most fundamental or general concepts and principles involved in thought, action and reality (Mautner 2005 p. 466)' (Hand, p. 10). Hand concludes that children *can* philosophize, for his claim is that doing philosophy basically amounts to conceptual analysis.

Hand's restriction of 'doing philosophy' to 'conceptual analysis' is a firm limitation on the kind of discussion that might count as philosophy. Catherine McCall, who has worked extensively training teachers to do philosophy with children, advocates the creation of a 'Community of Philosophical Inquiry' (CoPI) (2009) and states clearly what is to count as appropriate philosophical discussion. She is adamant that a chair (teacher) with philosophical training is necessary to steer any discussion towards explicit philosophical reasoning. She rules out the idea of individual 'musings' or wondering by explaining that here is no place for these in 'realist philosophy', which forms the basis of CoPI. Instead, she explains, discussion should focus on 'the philosophical assumptions and principles that underlie actions, judgement, emotions, etc.—distinguishing between epistemology, metaphysics, ethics, philosophy of mind, philosophy of science, etc.' (McCall, 2009, p. 94).

Critical thinking programmes for schools frequently echo the procedures that we might recognize as philosophizing: 'The underlying concern of critical thinking is the making of reasoned judgements and arriving at reasoned judgements in actual contexts of disagreement and debate is a dialectical process involving the comparative weighting and balancing of a variety of contending positions and arguments' (Bailin & Battersby, 2010). Critical thinking here is not seen as a series of mechanical techniques and strategies, but rather the actual process of arriving at judgements through inquiry is carefully and imaginatively shown to involve reason, skill and balance akin to disciplined philosophizing (Bailin & Battersby, 2011).

All three examples above are concerned with restricting, and therefore teaching, a particular and structured form of articulated reasoning that constitutes philosophy's educational value. However, Matthew Lipman's original idea of philosophical discussion to enhance children's thinking, together with some of the programmes such as SAPERE that were inspired by him, seem to stand in something of a contrast to these particular prescriptive accounts of what is educational about philosophy.

Catherine McCall believes that that Lipman's emphasis in P4C on a community of inquiry arises from the Deweyan emphasis on education for democracy where a 'respectful, caring and collaborative environment' offers a 'democratic practice in which children are joint creators of meaning' (McCall, 2009, p. 104). In particular, each child's experience and expression of their thinking is to have equal value regardless of its philosophical strength. Lipman's form of doing philosophy with children aims to generate critical, creative and caring thinking, rather than more disciplined, philosophical thinking, in contrast to McCall's allegiance to rigorous (realist) philosophical thought. CoPI aspires to teach children how to philosophize in a disciplined way, but the discipline is there to enable children to negotiate a link between the ideas of others and their own experience. This 'freer' model of discussion stems not just from Dewey's notion of democracy but from a much fuller account of Dewey's distinctive idea of education as experience.

The Deweyan emphasis on arriving at meaning through philosophical discussion in schools is identified by Judith Suissa (2008) as the significant pragmatist shift from truth to meaning. However, she observes that some versions of philosophical discussion in schools are beset by the problem of still seeing the pursuit of truth as the fundamental point of doing philosophy. She reminds us of Dewey's words:

poetic meanings, moral meanings, a large part of the goods of life are matters of richness and freedom of meaning, rather than of truth; a large part
of our life is carried on in a realm of meanings to which truth and falsity as
such are irrelevant. (Dewey, in Hickman & Alexander, 1998, p. 91)

Suissa allows that although some versions of critical thinking may encourage the
pursuit of truth and meaning, philosophy's capacity to develop critical thinking skills
or dispositions is not sufficient for it to have a place in the curriculum since 'surely
good teaching in any curricular subject is such that it encourages critical thinking'
(Suissa, 2008, p. 133). She concludes that philosophy should not become another
subject within the secondary school curriculum with all the assessment and curriculum guideline requirements that this would incur. Instead, she argues that classes in
philosophy might exist to engage children in speculative and imaginative exercises,
'loosely structured around the philosophical questions which arise from the aspects of
human life, culture and meaning encountered through the rest of the curriculum'
(Suissa, p. 143).

Philosophy and Literature

Other authors in Hand and Winstanley (2008) contend that literature and the arts
may provoke philosophical discussion within their subject frame. Karin Murris
describes and argues strongly for picture books to be used to provoke a form of philosophical discussion with young children. Chapters by Conroy and by Glueck and
Brighouse are less concerned with making discussion systematically philosophical, and
are more concerned to highlight the space that already exists for philosophical thought
within the study of literature. Murris is concerned to *use* the attributes of good picture
books in the service of philosophy, while Conroy is looking for educational sources
for cultivating wisdom and Glueck and Brighouse want teachers to be 'sensitive to,
and alert their students to, the philosophical dimensions' already present in much of
children's literature (Glueck & Brighouse, 2008, p. 119).

There is a clear sense that we are moving away from any promotion of children philosophizing to specifically learn to *do* philosophy from their own experiences: instead
the ability to philosophize is retained more straightforwardly, as an educationally valid
way of thinking. Ironically, Howard Gardner's classical work on multiple intelligences
offers 'existential intelligence' as closest to a philosophical intelligence, having dis-
carded 'logic' as too abstract. However, his own empiricist criteria for what counts as
an 'intelligence' force him to exclude it from an educational programme:

my hesitation in declaring a full-blown existential intelligence comes from
the dearth, so far, of evidence that parts of the brain are concerned particularly with these deep issues of existence ... it is possible that existential
questions are just part of a broader philosophical mind—or that they are
simply the more emotionally laden of the questions that individuals routinely pose. (Gardner, 2006b, p. 21)

In his desire to promote and articulate what he calls 'an education for understanding' Gardner later offers, echoing Lipman, a more developed and practically oriented view:

> It is possible to envision an education that assumes ... an approach ... rooted in the progressive tradition of John Dewey ... (where) the curriculum is built from the first, around gritty central questions or generative issues ... that thoughtful human beings all over the world have posed. (Gardner, 2006a, p. 148)

Gardner suggests that these issues might be introduced from an early age, through themes that reflect aspects of disciplinary inquiry in different conceptual domains such as 'identity and history' or 'the biological world'.

Some Educational Limitations

Michael Hand describes three popular misconceptions about philosophy that suggest that philosophy is a hard subject, beyond the understanding of many, especially primary school children. His first target is the idea that philosophy has no right or wrong answers, a claim which often appears in the statements of teachers who advocate the practice of doing philosophy with children. However, this seems an overly simplistic representation of the spirit behind the P4C movement in general. In the UK, teachers of young children have been, and many are still, hamstrung by a tightly objectives-led curriculum underpinned by a poor conceptualization of what counts as knowledge (Alexander, 2009, p. 247). Thoughtful primary teachers see in philosophy for children a way of teaching that does not have heavily prescribed and predetermined outcomes. The claim of 'no right or wrong answers' is arguably an exaggeration of this characteristic and a false dichotomy. The sense of freedom from prescription could be what underpins their professional excitement at finding a way of teaching that allows for a variety of answers to count as appropriate. As Murris puts it:

> many teachers and pupils have become dependent upon the certainty of right and wrong answers and feel lost and confused when questions elude simple resolution. They have become victims of a mostly answers-based curriculum that offers an ill-founded sense of security (Haynes & Murris 2006). (Murris, 2008, p. 115)

It is not that there are no right or wrong answers in philosophy but that philosophical discussion avoids simplistically assessable answers. In philosophy, and even with quite young children, answers or responses put forward can be questioned, unpacked, developed and elaborated in subtle ways that much of the current UK primary curriculum content does not allow for.

Hand implies that many of the P4C programmes are happy to raise questions in ways that suggest that philosophers have failed to make any progress over 'perennial' dilemmas. He dismisses this misconception by explaining how conceptual analysis allows for the tracing of 'logical implications of possible uses of particular concepts' (Hand, 2008, p. 10). Indeed, many of Lipman's games map out concept maps, requiring children to consider necessary and sufficient conditions for the use of a word, but more are open to disagreement or argument. Questions such as 'How do we know when something is fair?' or 'Is kindness enough to make anyone a good person?' can provoke a new direction for puzzlement, a depth of thought and reflection that for those encountering the exploration of such ideas for the first time, creates felt originality, freshness and excitement. While many of the questions are framed from the writings of different philosophers over time, there is no need to be aware of the historical context of the use of a concept to encourage those involved in the discussion to think through what such a question might entail or mean for oneself or where discrepancies and contradictions arise in understanding.

A more apposite point comes from Glueck and Brighouse:

> Philosophical discussion can be especially difficult to manage, because it must be somewhat open-ended in order for it to elicit genuinely philosophical thinking, but it must not leave the impression that everyone's opinion is as valid as everyone else's or that there are no truths at stake. Because if that were so the activity of critical reasoning would be pointless. (Glueck & Brighouse, 2008, p. 130)

This brief summary of accounts of philosophy with children begins with the more prescribed or narrow views of what counts as doing philosophy and ends with the broader view, that the philosophical ideas and thinking which pervade our lives can be valuable when made explicit in already legitimized educational domains. While the earlier characterizations stress the need for specific philosophical training, the latter ideas suggest that philosophical thought can exist and be encouraged as a more generalized feature of education. Each account suggests some tension between the individual and social experience of language, and between creative imagination and rigid structure, and a Deweyan perspective may resolve the tension by appealing to pragmatic judgement.

The Influence of Dewey

The claim embedded in some philosophy for children programmes, that meaning accrued through social encounters is of educational value because it is a way of developing of self-knowledge, is not adequate to give philosophy a place in the curriculum. Suissa (2008, p. 136) argues that Dewey's stress on experience is far richer and 'rooted in the idea that humans are essentially concerned with a constant attempt to make and to improve shared meanings out of their active encounter with the natural, social and cultural worlds' (Suissa, p. 138).

The stress on communication and participation in education as features of associated living is vital for Dewey's conceptualization of education and democracy. As Gert Biesta has pointed out:

> The central notion in pragmatism's philosophy of communication is the idea of participation, because it is participation—and, more specifically

real, not pseudo-participation—which has the potential to contribute to the creation of a shared world. (Biesta, 2010, p. 724)

The stress on personal meaning, then, is not at the expense of participation and community. An appetite for educational experience is necessarily generated and embedded in shared communication in its many forms. Because Dewey's fundamental educational ideas do rest in his complex conceptualization of 'experience' and community, the supposed promotion of democracy, by, for example, simple turn-taking, is found to be inadequate as an argument for doing philosophy in schools. The imperative in Dewey's work is to closely address the quality of any engagement deemed educational. In the particular focus here on communication in the form of open-ended discussions, participants create meaning for themselves through both listening to others and becoming more conscious of their own thoughts and ideas as they contribute, so that 'talk may not merely serve to articulate the emotional and reflective life, but actually constitute it' (Doddington, 2001, p. 272).

Dewey's influence is not about advocating some form of intellectual debating exercise and at the same time discussion is not merely an exchange of views, for 'there is more at stake (in the processes of communication) than the simple exchange of different perspectives on the same reality' (Biesta, 2010, p. 725). For Dewey, that the views expressed are *personally* meaningful is vital for experience to be educational. Concerns introduced should be real and puzzles should be genuine if children are to authentically invest themselves in communication. Personal involvement is vital because it creates conditions that will encourage children to *want to* reflect in collaboration with others or, in Dewey's phrase, be 'ready' 'to consider in a thoughtful way the subjects that do come within the range of experience—a readiness that contrasts strongly with the disposition to pass judgement on the basis of mere custom, tradition, prejudice, etc., and thus shun the task of thinking' (Dewey, 1989, p. 139).

If we are to grasp the Deweyan notion of being ready to experience in an educational sense, we need to understand what might constitute 'readiness'. This is akin to certain dispositions that prepare us to be receptive to encounters, and Dewey lists four attributes: open-mindedness, whole-heartedness, responsibility and, later, directness, as the 'moral traits' (Dewey, 1985, pp. 366–367) that are necessary to prepare us to learn through communicative encounters. Open-mindedness for Dewey has an active quality and denotes a willingness to consider the new and the unfamiliar: 'an open-minded person merges curiosity, wonder and respect into an active receptivity to new points of view, to new outlooks and to new ways of thinking and knowing' (Hanson, 2006, p. 170). This openness warns against predetermined communications or prejudgements, suggesting that space is needed for 'the intervention of what cannot be foreseen; the intervention of the other' (Biesta, 2010, p. 734). Whole-heartedness describes the desire and willingness to fully engage, standing in contrast to a half-hearted approach to an encounter. A 'whole-hearted individual remains absorbed, immersed, engrossed and as best as possible sees the activity or task through to completion' (Hanson, p. 170). Being responsible implies facing the challenge of working through what emerges in an encounter to see what difference it makes to one's present, personal understandings and beliefs, while directness implies having the courage to be clear-sighted in focusing one's energies and resources well.

Suissa reminded us that a Deweyan view of 'experience' should direct an individual's attention towards the betterment of the social condition, and these four dispositions reassert the significance for the individual, not just for self-knowledge, but for a quality of experience that can 'fund the self in substantial ways, fuelling its growth so that in all subsequent situations it has greater resources and energies to bring to bear, thereby generating an ascending spiral of experience and quality of life' (Hanson, 2006, p. 173).

Philosophy as Wonder

Doing philosophy through discussion can contribute to authentic language experiences in school through which 'both personal and cultural identity can be forged' (Doddington, 2001, p. 269) through openness, whole-heartedness, engagement and responsibility in a synergy which creates meaning. These are related, especially if we conceive of responsibility in the Buberian sense of responding, to another significant feature of philosophy that turns us outward, to look beyond ourselves—that of wonder. Plato argues that the 'feeling of wonder is very characteristic of the philosopher' and that 'philosophy has no other starting point …' (Plato, *Theaetetus 155d*), while Aristotle suggests 'it was because of wonder that men both now and originally began to philosophise' (Aristotle, *Metaphysics 982b*) (in Mackenzie, 2008, p. 5). This refers to a wider and older notion of philosophical contemplation and wonderings and yet with the idea of children engaging with philosophy, it regains some significance. Children can express delight and amazement at simple things and we could argue that many childlike questions such as 'Where did the moon come from?' or even 'Why should I be good?' show that, necessarily, through their lack of experience and understanding about the world, there is a natural tendency to 'wonder'. The temptation to launch into explanations for these questions when children pose them can be great for any parent or teacher as a simple desire to inform and educate. However, Dewey would require that to be truly educational, any form of response should not close down the enquiry with an answer, but should preserve and inspire further capacity to wonder. However we conceptualize the role of the educator here, the space to play with thoughts is necessary, the release from 'correctness' and 'preordained' answers and the ability for teachers to show 'children that utterances can be "food for thought" rather than prompts for interrogation' (Doddington, 2001, p. 273) are important. And before the criticism occurs that this just characterizes a comfortable 'armchair' activity, it is worth saying that in a Deweyan sense, 'an open-minded attitude is one that never takes anything for granted and continuously questions assumptions. Philosophical puzzlement is an emotional condition involving doubt and uncertainty. It may give rise to feelings of alienation, despair or excitement' (Haynes, 2008, p. 42).

Philosophy and Beyond

If the kinds of exchanges I have sketched qualify as philosophizing and wonder is seen as central, philosophy as a community of inquiry has certain qualities in common with other kinds of engagement and communication in, for example, the arts and literature. In both philosophizing and artistic engagements, there needs to be some freedom from the imperatives of the urgent or mundane. Similar to the idea of playing a game, receptivity and open-mindedness allow the participants to submit to a co-constructed situation or shared conceptualization and in a reflective, unprescribed context of a sustained activity or discussion, teachers and children are able to 'play with ideas' and wonder, or imagine—they can entertain possibilities. However, it is important to stress that the notion of play used here is a serious one, whereby 'the structure of play absorbs the player into itself and thus frees him from the burden of taking the initiative which constitutes the actual strain of existence' (Gadamer, 1989, p. 105).

Philosophical discussion, the reading of literature and encounters with other art forms are examples of forms of engagement that are characterized by a freedom to wonder and by a lack of thought centred on direct action or necessity. They can be distinguished from encounters with the world that function to provide quick practical solutions or basic survival needs. It is by approaching an event or object in this non-instrumental way that an individual can in some 'playful' sense be released from normal everyday constraints to imagine and see beyond the particularity of the present to create meaning. These characteristics can be applied more broadly—to the educational experience of children engaging in *making* art, for example:

> Each of us, as artist, can take what is common and shared, and through art, shape and form it to return it to the world made *meaningful* through the personal lens that is distinctive to us as an individual. This emphasis in making art stresses that children's immediate, personal experiences are the rich source from which they can return their impressions to the world in imaginative ways. (Doddington, 2010, p. 586)

By now, the notion of philosophy appears to be evaporating from the argument and Suissa's complaint about an interpretation of Dewey's 'experience' leaving too narrow a focus on the individual has pertinence again. Yet my intention is not to eclipse philosophy or fall into an individualistic self-knowledge trap, but to step back to see what various expressions of Deweyan experience as education may ultimately have in common with art. Hanson's description of involvement that enriches and promotes experience could apply to both a particular version of philosophizing and other ways of engaging with others. 'The more the self can infuse into a situation, the richer the situation and the richer the possible incremental transformation of the self—this will be much more assured if situations increasingly feature greater infusions from the world by way of objects, including other selves enjoying a comparable experience' (Hanson, 2006, p. 173).

To link the argument back to philosophical questions, it is necessary to see how Dewey emphasizes that educational experience should generate 'moral knowledge' that 'builds up a social interest and confers the intelligence needed to make that interest effective in practice' (Dewey, 1985, p. 366). The term 'moral knowledge' is used

> to capture what students and teachers learn through activities that are saturated with interaction between themselves and the most challenging subject

matter they are equipped to tackle ... (where) they learn that ideas, inter-pretations, explanations and ways of knowing have consequences ... are *alive* ... are part of *their* lives and they expand the scene of life. (Hanson, 2006, p. 183)

For Dewey, understanding across the curriculum is acquired 'under conditions where ... social significance is realised' (Dewey, 1985, p. 366) and in ways that 'feed moral interest and develop moral insight' (Dewey, 1985, p. 366). It seems that while it is central to philosophy, the question 'How should we live our lives?' can also be broached through a range of learning engagements.

While many arguments for philosophy with children rest on the work of Dewey, a return to some of the subtleties and complexity in his work gives a richer idea of how this might be best manifest in school. Philosophy with children can offer this quality of communication but other educational encounters can be designed to achieve similar experiences. A Deweyan view actually allows for different manifestations of the kinds of experience he deems educational, including literature. There is no doubt that in a very practical sense, teachers may see in children philosophizing, a fresh approach and a contrast to performative, objectives-led learning and teaching, and therefore a welcome relief from the current education mantras of 'pace' and 'curriculum cover-age'. In addition, it could be argued that the range of philosophy with children pro-grammes at least offers protected opportunity and time for philosophizing in ways that support a systematic development of the capacity to reflect in a distinctively philosophical way.

However, one question remains. If the desirables we see highlighted by Dewey's notion of 'experience' are not exclusive and are achievable in a variety of ways, to what extent are they *best* achieved through philosophy for children? My suggestion has been that philosophy for children is but one, well-supported way of achieving that quality of experience and that other subjects, especially art, may well suffice to provide wonder and meaning.

The Significance of Pedagogy

My final point in this argument is that if teachers understand the qualities of educa-tional experience they wish to pursue, consciously look for or intentionally create, *they* might recognize that this quality of collaborative experience may occur through phi-losophy for children, but not only there. It can occur elsewhere, including through communication centred on poetry, drama, picture books, visual art, and moral or civic dilemmas. Perhaps more significantly, consciousness of this desirable state of experience for children implies that it can, and probably should, be present more gen-erally in the classroom as a community, and in a more pervasive sense than simply the weekly lesson or incidental discussion. It needs to be a feature of the ongoing tri-adic relationship between students, teachers and the curriculum, and in this way, become an inherent part of the pedagogy of teachers, occurring whenever it is oppor-tune, as well as when it is planned for. Working towards this form of educational experience, then, should become a consistent characteristic of a teacher's repertoire for teaching. It could be argued that the extent of prescription that teachers are accustomed to means that some of the philosophy programmes discussed above offer the surest and most practical way of allowing this at least to happen regularly. However, steering existing discussion and collaboration in the arts and through literature to create an appetite for wonder and engagement may suffice. We should also be arguing for more professional understanding and autonomy for teachers in the practice and characterization of their pedagogy. This autonomy, alongside a whole-hearted commitment to creating a high-quality educational experience, may allow teachers themselves to exercise judgement about when, where and how philosophizing with children in any of its many forms could most fruitfully happen in schools, and thus constitute for children a community for rich educational experience, heralded and conceptualized by John Dewey.

References

Alexander, R. (2009). *Children, their world, their education: Final report and recommendations of the Cambridge Primary Review*. London: Routledge.

Bailin, S., & Battersby, M. (2010, July). Reasoned judgement, comparative evaluation, and the balancing of considerations. Presented at the INPE Conference, Universidad de Los Andes, Bogota, Columbia.

Bailin, S., & Battersby, M. (2011). *Reason in the balance. An inquiry approach to critical thinking*. Whitby, Canada: McGraw-Hill Ryerson.

Benade, L. (2010). Book review. *Educational Philosophy and Theory, 42*, 808–811.

Biesta, G. (2010). This is my truth, tell me yours. Deconstructive pragmatism as a philosophy for education. *Educational Philosophy and Theory, 42*, 710–727.

Conroy, J. (2008). Philosophy, wisdom and reading great books. In M. Hand & C. Winstanley (Eds.), *Philosophy in schools* (pp. 145–157). London: Continuum.

Dewey, J. (1985). Democracy and education. In J. A. Boydston (Ed.) (2008). *The later works, 1925–1953*, Vol. 9, *Democracy and education 1916* (pp. 4–356). Carbondale, IL: Southern Illinois University Press.

Dewey, J. (1989). How we think. In J. A. Boydston (Ed.) (2008). *The later works, 1925–1953*, Vol. 8, *Essays and 'How we think'* (pp. 105–353). Carbondale, IL: Southern Illinois University Press.

Doddington, C. (2001). Entitled to speak: Talk in the classroom. *Studies in Philosophy and Education, 20*, 267–274.

Doddington, C. (2010). Mimesis and experience revisited: Can philosophy revive the practice of arts education? *Journal of Philosophy of Education of Great Britain, 44*, 579–587.

Fisher, R. (2003). *Teaching thinking: Philosophical enquiry in the classroom* (2nd ed.). London: Continuum.

Fisher, R. (2008). Philosophical intelligence. In M. Hand & C. Winstanley (Eds.), *Philosophy in schools* (pp. 96–114). London: Continuum.

Gaarder, J. (1995). *Sophie's world*. London: Phoenix House.

Gadamer, H.G. (1989). *Truth & method*. London: Sheed & Ward.

Gardner, H. (2006a). *The development and education of the mind*. Abingdon: Routledge.

Gardner, H. (2006b). *New horizons*. New York: Basic Books.

Glueck, L., & Brighouse, H. (2008). Philosophy in children's literature. In M. Hand & C. Winstanley (Eds.), *Philosophy in schools* (pp. 119–131). London: Continuum.

Hand, M. (2008). Can children be taught philosophy? In M. Hand & C. Winstanley (Eds.), *Philosophy in schools* (pp. 3–17). London: Continuum.

Hand, M., & Winstanley, C. (Eds.). (2008). *Philosophy in schools*. London: Continuum.

Hanson, D. (Ed.). (2006). *John Dewey and our educational prospect*. Albany, NY: State University of New York Press.

Haynes, J. (2008). *Children as philosophers: Learning through enquiry and dialogue in the primary classroom* (2nd ed.). London: Routledge.

Hickman, L. & Alexander, T. (Eds). (1998). *The essential Dewey: Volume 2. Ethics, logic, psychology*. Indiana: Indiana University Press.

Lipman, M. (2003). *Thinking in education* (2nd ed.). Cambridge: Cambridge University Press.

Mackenzie, R. (2008, April). Philosophy and education as compassion and wonder. Paper presented at the Philosophy of Education Society of Great Britain's Annual Conference, Oxford.

McCall, C. (2009). *Transforming thinking: philosophical inquiry in the primary and secondary classroom*. London: Routledge.

Murris, K. (2008). Autonomous and authentic thinking through philosophy with picturebooks. In M. Hand & C. Winstanley (Eds.), *Philosophy in schools* (pp. 105–118). London: Continuum.

Suissa, J. (2008). Philosophy in the secondary school—A Deweyan perspective. In M. Hand & C. Winstanley (Eds.), *Philosophy in schools* (pp. 132–144). London: Continuum.

Winstanley, C. (2008). Philosophy and the development of critical thinking. In M. Hand & C. Winstanley (Eds.), *Philosophy in schools* (pp. 85–95). London: Continuum.

Kaupapa Māori, Philosophy and Schools

GEORGINA STEWART

Faculty of Education, University of Auckland,

Abstract

Goals for adding philosophy to the school curriculum centre on the perceived need to improve the general quality of critical thinking found in society. School philosophy also provides a means for asking questions of value and purpose about curriculum content across and between subjects, and, furthermore, it affirms the capability of children to think philosophically. Two main routes suggested are the introduction of philosophy as a subject, and processes of facilitating philosophical discussions as a way of establishing classroom 'communities of inquiry'. This article analyses the place of philosophy in the school curriculum, drawing on three relevant examples of school curriculum reform: social studies, philosophy of science and Kura Kaupapa Māori.

Introduction

The work of Matthew Lipman in the 1970s (see http://plato.stanford.edu/entries/children; www.p4c.org.nz) encouraged the promotion of philosophy in schools. Goals for adding philosophy to the school curriculum centre on the perceived need to improve the general quality of critical thinking found in society. School philosophy also provides a means for asking questions of value and purpose about curriculum content across and between subjects, and, furthermore, it affirms the capability of children to think philosophically (with the implication that this has previously been in doubt). However, philosophy is not currently part of the national school curriculum in Aotearoa New Zealand (Ministry of Education, 2007, 2008).

The two main ways of promoting philosophy in schools are the introduction of philosophy as a subject and processes of facilitating philosophical discussions as a way of establishing classroom 'communities of inquiry'. Two prevalent concerns about this idea are that the school curriculum is already overloaded with subjects and content, and that there are doubts that teachers know enough about philosophy to be confident or competent in teaching it. The question of including philosophy in the school curriculum is discussed in this article with the aim of focusing on some less widely acknowledged possibilities and limitations of this apparently worthy tradition of curricular reform. The discussion draws in turn on three relevant examples of school curriculum reform: social studies, philosophy of science and Kura Kaupapa Māori (KKM).

Social Studies Curriculum Reform for Critical Thinking

The first question concerns the novelty or otherwise of the declared goals of introducing philosophy into the school curriculum. The assertion that these are original goals is not supported by the literature on curriculum history. Social studies originated in the mid-twentieth century from very similar considerations to those currently expressed by advocates of school philosophy. One of its three major traditions is defined as 'reflective inquiry, where the emphasis is on pupils selecting the issues and problems themselves and evolving decisions through critical thinking' (Openshaw, 1996, p. 163).

Is philosophy in the curriculum therefore designed to take over this function, as an offshoot of social studies, similar to the evolution of media studies out of English? This question is posed in a ludic spirit, given the lack of suggestion in the literature on philosophy in schools that such is the case. Nevertheless, given the intersection between their stated goals, the history of social studies may well be relevant to the future prospects of philosophy. The literature documents an ongoing struggle to compete against the more traditional subjects such as mathematics and science, and to resolve its internal conflicts into a clear, universally accepted rationale. There is little evidence of success in operationalizing the ideals of open reflective inquiry on which social studies was founded.

The primary cause of these struggles lies in the fact that school curriculum is a site of contest between the aims and discourses of diverse groups who seek to influence the direction of education, given its perceived role in shaping society's future. These debates have only become more polarized and explicit in recent decades (since 1990 in Aotearoa New Zealand), in moving away from centralization towards a 'contractualist' process of curriculum development (Openshaw, 1996). The resulting curricula therefore embody political compromises, or perhaps more to the point, political solutions found by state agencies to unresolved conflicts between educational stakeholders. In this way, the contestation process drives the curriculum towards a conservative, apparently 'value-free' outcome, which militates against achieving the sorts of goals with which advocates for philosophy (or, indeed, social studies) are concerned.

But such goals are not restricted to social studies within the framework of the existing school curriculum. Calls for increased relevance to modern society have been influencing school curriculum development for around a century now, to move beyond or away from its origins in the 'traditional academic disciplines' (Openshaw, Clark, Hamer, & Waitere-Ang, 2005, p. 193). School curriculum reform in the twentieth century has been characterized as containing three traditions, each arguably at odds with the others: the social efficiency movement, the child-centred movement, and the social meliorists. The latter movement 'believed that the curriculum should encourage students to challenge and critique what they saw around them in the interests of creating a more just society' (Openshaw et al., 2005, p. 163). In other words, the stated goal of improving critical thinking for social justice applies not just to existing subjects, but to the school curriculum as a whole.

In broad-brush terms, through the middle part of the twentieth century, social studies was charged with responsibility for these social meliorist goals, but in today's curriculum, every subject claims to play a role in which each of these three traditions is recognizable. For example, mathematics education includes in its rationale the need for modern citizens to understand statistics about society; science education draws attention to the need for informed social debate on science issues; English points to the crucial role of literacy in democratic participation, and so on. The newer subjects of health, technology and education for sustainability are even more strongly under-pinned by rationales of personal development and social improvement, as opposed to traditional disciplinary knowledge.

Besides the subjects themselves, today's school curriculum has an increasingly important 'front end' specifying generic goals expressed as sets of principles, values and key competencies, which schools are expected to engender in students through the curriculum. The descriptors 'critical and creative thinkers' and 'informed decision makers' appear in the statement titled 'Vision: What we want for our young people' at the start of the New Zealand Curriculum (Ministry of Education, 2007, p. 8). The role envisaged for philosophy in schools has clearly already been thoroughly rehearsed, which minimizes any likelihood that this rationale for including philosophy in the curriculum will meet with success.

Philosophy of Science in Science Curricular Reform

If the process-oriented goals for philosophy in schools are insufficiently novel or dis-tinctive, advocates might still wish to argue for including philosophical disciplinary knowledge; in other words, philosophy as a subject. Yet this move seems perilously close to falling into the very trap from which the school curriculum has for many years been trying to escape, that of justifying curriculum content on the grounds of its inherent value as knowledge. The older or starting-point orientation towards curriculum 'as a fixed and traditional body of knowledge' succumbs to the weaknesses of epistemic transcendence or universality, and ignores the changes that have taken place in epistemology since around 1900. As mainstream academic philosophy continues to struggle to overcome its lack of historical reflexivity, to redefine itself beyond the end of metaphysics and in response to the linguistic, cultural and narrative turns of the twentieth century and beyond (Peters, 2011), there seems more danger than promise in the attempt to inaugurate a 'body of knowledge' as the subject of philosophy in the school curriculum.

The source and nature of this 'danger' are made apparent by the broader contemporary understanding of school curriculum, labelled 'the pedagogical view' (Openshaw et al., 2005, p. 188). This view recognizes the biases, distortions, embedded discourses and silences that contribute to the 'hidden curriculum'—the unavoidable companion to that which is set out in official curriculum documents, and with considerable influence in the outcomes of school education. For philosophy, the hidden curriculum amounts to an ideological burden resting on questions such as *whose* philosophy might be taught, and which cultural, gender and class perspectives might be privileged in so doing. These questions echo those used to challenge the selection of curricular content in other subjects, with science being a case in point.

The history of the science curriculum documents particularly intransigent debates concerning the philosophy of the subject, and its nature as a form of knowledge. No other school curriculum area has been more concerned with the philosophy *of* the subject; nor had greater difficulty meeting the challenges of diversity—especially cultural diversity—in recent decades (Siegel, 2002).

Science is a good example of what happens when distorted representations of the subject are portrayed in the school curriculum. The term 'school science' is widely used to refer to these overly reductionist, simplistic versions of science (Aikenhead, 2000). Such 'myths about science' also include misogynist, racist and scientistic overtones (Hodson, 1999). The phenomenon of 'school science' acts to perpetuate societal ignorance and misunderstandings about the nature and philosophy of science, with an ultimately impoverishing influence on science itself. No amount of curricular rhetoric can conceal the extent to which science education still acts as a gatekeeper for the wealthy in terms of access to higher education and the professions in our society today (McKinley, 2008). These trends show little if any sign of changing, despite pressure on schools and teachers to take measures such as adopting culturally responsive pedagogies (Bishop, Berryman, Cavanagh, & Teddy, 2007).

In a recent article, a long-time advocate for teaching philosophy of science in science education attributes his support in part to the influence on his views of Lipman's Philosophy for Children (Davson-Galle, 2008, p. 677). Davson-Galle makes a careful examination of the possible justifications for teaching philosophy of science (to various degrees of complexity and active engagement) as part of the compulsory secondary school science curriculum. He weighs the possible benefits (extrinsic or intrinsic) to the individual student, or to the group, of these various degrees of compulsory teaching of philosophy of science (both epistemic and ethical issues), against the cost of the loss of freedom of choice suffered by the entire populations of students involved. After thorough discussion, he reaches a pessimistic conclusion:

> As far as I can work out, beyond a possible warrant for the most basic 'Nature of Science' sense of 'an introduction', it is hard to see enough benefit of any sort, for the individual, or for the rest of us, to outweigh the loss of student choice as to what is learnt. (Davson-Galle, 2008, p. 708)

Davson-Galle bases the strength of his argument on the 'observation [that] compulsory schooling is a sustained exercise in force in which individual freedom of action and freedom of thought are interfered with' (p. 684). The argument of his article is that there is an ethical contradiction in the situation where all future citizens, who have the right to be treated as 'free agents', are nevertheless compelled to 'learn' ethics. In closing he notes, 'although narrowly focused upon philosophy of science, [much] the same sort of freedom-valuing onus argument would seem to apply to other parts of the compulsory curriculum' (p. 708). In particular, these objections apply to any suggestion that philosophy *per se* become part of the compulsory curriculum.

This provides a specific example of the processes of the 'hidden curriculum' at work. Davson-Galle (2008) draws attention to the paradox of how curricular reforms seeking to improve social equity break against the bedrock criteria of universal human rights, on which the ethical basis for state education rests. Given due consideration of the inherent discursive processes of curriculum, there is little scope for politically innocent expectations of philosophy in schools.

Philosophy and Kura Kaupapa Māori

Disillusionment with the extent and efficacy of reforms within the mainstream school system to address historical inequity for Māori in education was a contributing factor in the efforts to establish a separate school system, namely Kura Kaupapa Māori (KKM) (Sharples, 1994). The relevance to this discussion is that 'kaupapa' encompasses the meaning of 'philosophy'. (Tellingly enough, it also simultaneously means 'political cause'.) The case of KKM and its underlying philosophy of 'kaupapa Māori' forms the third and final specific example against which to discuss the prospects for philosophy in the school curriculum.

As noted above, the second half of the twentieth century was a time of increasing awareness of the human and group rights of cultural minorities in Western societies. In Aotearoa New Zealand, there was a new level of acknowledgement concerning the historical disadvantages suffered by Māori people, and the role played by schools in advancing these inequities. Despite expressed positive will, however, changes for Māori in the mainstream education system in the 1970s and 1980s were neither substantive nor rapid enough to accommodate the process of widespread political conscientizing of Māori people and their resulting cultural, political and economic aspirations (Smith, 1990, 2002). The monocultural system presented structural impediments to Māori aspirations, which ensured the failure of Māori educational policy reforms to meet the needs of Māori individuals and communities (Smith, 1991).

The emergence of autonomous Māori educational reform efforts, in particular Te Kohanga Reo and KKM, was in response to these frustrations. KKM are schools 'based on Kaupapa Māori philosophy' (Smith, 1991, p. 18). Kaupapa Māori philosophy is a critical, culturally specific philosophy that underpins an overall orientation towards education. The key point about KKM, which could not be achieved within the mainstream education system, is that it represents a structural intervention. It embodies the recognition that, in education, philosophy goes beyond the curriculum to permeate all structures and practices of the school at every level. But to describe the situation in these terms recalls the previous discussion concerning the wider, pedagogical view of curriculum:

> embod[ying] the broader social, political and cultural processes or constructs which embrace values, assumptions, fundamental beliefs about the world, basic knowledge and visions of utopias ... it is not an object to be

transmitted but a socially constructed set of shared understandings set within, and influenced by, the social and policy contexts of education. (Openshaw et al., 2005, p. 188)

The establishment of KKM as culturally based school systems can thus be conceived within a wider consideration of school curriculum reform. It brings us back, in conclusion, to the question: Who is envisaged to benefit from the introduction of philosophy into the school curriculum? If KKM are based on Māori philosophies, then mainstream schools must be based on Western philosophies, and the philosophy proposed for inclusion in the school curriculum is by extension an implicitly Western philosophy. Without critical reflection on the inherent Eurocentrism in the existing school curriculum, calls for the introduction of philosophy in schools serve only to further entrench the cultural bias of the hidden curriculum. The method of community of inquiry would seem to present a more culturally responsive way to introduce critical thinking in school than the traditional subject of Philosophy.

References

Aikenhead, G. (2000). Renegotiating the culture of school science. In R. Millar, J. Leach, & J. Osborne (Eds.), *Improving science education—The contribution of research* (pp. 245–264). Buckingham: Open University Press.

Bishop, R., Berryman, M., Cavanagh, T., & Teddy, L. (2007). *Te Kotahitanga phase 3: Establishing a culturally responsive pedagogy of relations in mainstream secondary school classrooms.* Wellington: Ministry of Education.

Davson-Galle, P. (2008). Why compulsory science education should *not* include philosophy of science. *Science & Education, 17,* 677–716.

Hodson, D. (1999). Critical multiculturalism in science and technology education. In S. May (Ed.), *Critical multiculturalism: Rethinking multicultural and antiracist education* (pp. 216–244). London: Falmer Press.

McKinley, E. (2008). Māori in science and mathematics education. In J. S. Te Rito & S. M. Healy (Eds.), *Te ara pūtaiao: Māori insights in science.* Auckland: Ngā Pae o te Māramatanga.

Ministry of Education. (2007). *The New Zealand curriculum.* Wellington: Learning Media.

Ministry of Education. (2008). *Te marautanga o Aotearoa.* Wellington: Learning Media.

Openshaw, R. (1996). Social studies in the curriculum? Critical citizenship or crucial cop out? *Delta, 48*(2), 159–172.

Openshaw, R., Clark, J., Hamer, J., & Waitere-Ang, H. (2005). Contesting the curriculum in Aotearoa New Zealand. In P. Adams, R. Openshaw, & J. Hamer (Eds.), *Education and society in Aotearoa New Zealand* (2nd ed., pp. 187–224). Southbank, Vic.: Thomson.

Peters, M. (2010). *The last book of postmodernism.* New York: Peter Lang.

Sharples, P. (1994). Kura Kaupapa Māori. In H. McQueen (Ed.), *Education is change* (pp. 11–21). Wellington: Bridget Williams Books.

Siegel, H. (2002). Multiculturalism, universalism, and science education: In search of common ground. *Science education, 86,* 803–820.

Smith, G. H. (1990). The politics of reforming Māori education: The transforming potential of Kura Kaupapa Māori. In H. Lauder & C. Wylie (Eds.), *Towards successful schooling* (pp. 73–87). London: Falmer Press.

Smith, G. H. (1991). *In absentia: Māori education policy and reform.* Wellington: NZCER.

Smith, G. H. (1997). *The development of Kaupapa Māori: Theory and praxis* (Unpublished PhD) University of Auckland, Auckland.

School and the Limits of Philosophy

PETER FITZSIMONS

Education & Management Services (NZ) Ltd

Abstract

Philosophy and schools, children and dynamite, elephants and postage stamps: each has a place, but not necessarily in any natural combination with the other. Whether schools and philosophy belong together depends largely on what we mean by both. To the extent that schools are instruments of government regulation and a mechanism for production of economic subjectivity, philosophy might be welcome as an ancillary technique for enhancing problem-solving skills or helping students to think more logically. If, on the other hand, teachers are concerned to promote education as the development of independent thought beyond the realm of instrumental utility, then philosophy is a vital, and potentially critical, engagement with power, with the way schools function, and more generally with society and its government. With reference to some recent policy moves in education, this article argues that the focus on the economic productivity of education is intensifying, and that as educational institutions become more heavily regulated and monitored, there is little provision for, or toleration of, any form of structural criticism, philosophical or otherwise. The conclusion is that philosophy may have an explicit place within the existing school programmes, but that any philosophy which provides a basis for fundamental change in our patterns and expectations of schooling is likely to be undermined. Commitment to critical philosophy becomes, then, a surreptitious activity on the part of individual teachers, operating outside the official curriculum and frustrated by increasing surveillance and demands for accountability.

Introduction

The word *philosophy* has become part of our everyday conversation. Some institutions, schools among them, are said to have a particular philosophy, meaning they are driven by a particular doctrine or system of beliefs accepted as authoritative within that institution. More generally, a *philosophy* might refer to a personal belief about how to live or how to deal with a situation, as in 'my philosophy is to let sleeping dogs lie'. The *Concise Oxford dictionary* reflects this variety of meanings, listing philosophy as including the use of reason and argument in seeking truth and knowledge of reality; and alternatively, as a personal rule of life or as advanced learning in general. To be 'philosophical' is to be wise, serene, temperate and calm in adverse circumstances. There is hope for us yet.

The *Oxford companion to philosophy* notes that what has been called philosophy has changed radically in scope over the course of history. The shortest definition provided is that philosophy is 'thinking about thinking', emphasizing the second order character of philosophy as reflective thought about particular kinds of thinking, beliefs and knowledge about the world or large parts of it. The same volume provides an extended definition, which is more detailed but represented as still 'uncontroversially comprehensive':

> Philosophy is rationally critical thinking, of a more or less systematic kind about the general nature of the world (metaphysics or theory of existence), the justification of belief (epistemology or theory of knowledge), and the conduct of life (ethics or theory of value). (Quinton, 1995, p. 666)

It is a challenge to work out what it is we are talking about when we refer to philosophy and schools. Neither this article nor the schools to which it refers can possibly encompass the full complexity of what is called philosophy. For the purposes of containment, then, this article will restrict its focus to (1) the deliberate introduction of philosophical content into school programmes, (2) the adoption of philosophical approaches to existing school curricula, and (3) the potential for philosophy to question the appropriation of the purposes and function of schools for political and economic ends. This last inclusion constitutes the thrust of this article: a call for critical engagement with various policy directions and legislative requirements that regulate participation in educational relationships. With similar self-determination, the article will expand the definition of schools to encompass a range of institutions generally considered to be educational, but which, it is argued, serve other purposes and functions in our society.

Schools are Constrained

Schools, by their nature and in their *raison d'être*, are constrained. Even at the linguistic level, the word 'school' has a number of nuances that go beyond simple reference to a building for educational engagement. A school of thought is a collection or group of people who share common characteristics of opinion or outlook, perhaps in terms of discipline, philosophy or belief. The process of schooling implies instruction or training rather than free exploration or engaging in personal pursuits. Further, our schools are explicitly designed for the intentional education of young people, as a form of enculturation, socialization and inculcation into the disciplined forms of thought that characterize Western knowledge production. Schooling in the broad sense (here including university education) is needed to extend and refine knowledge for a skilled workforce and ongoing research and development in a modern economy. A less explicit, but just as vital role, is the custodial function that schools serve, assembling and occupying vast numbers of young people in such a way that a teaching profession is kept employed, parents are liberated from child-minding and able to compete with the unemployed for jobs in the marketplace, and the students themselves are assessed and credentialled to legitimate certain forms of socioeconomic stratification and privilege. Our educational institutions, then, are focal points for the insertion of government policy, nodules in the networks of social and cultural subjectivity.

Because they are intricately interwoven with economic productivity, and because they are powerful mechanisms in the production of subjectivity, schools are characterized by a formal structure, within a disciplined ethos of accountability, and aligned with the vision of government—at both the macro- and micro-level, from the length and timing of a school year to the number of hours in a day; from the style and content of the curriculum to the mechanisms for its delivery; and from the physical environment of the school buildings to the monitoring of compulsory attendance.[1] Given the level of surveillance and external control of schools, it is not surprising to find a considerable degree of similarity across schools in both their programmes and their political acquiescence. Contributing to their homogeneity, a number of purportedly educational initiatives are now outlined—initiatives that reduce diversity and intensify compliance with government agendas, with nary a philosophical consideration in sight.

Recent Education Policy

In accord with broader policy directions, the Ministry of Education is intent upon accelerating academic achievement, promoting outputs that are measurable in terms of human capital, and disabling as far as acceptable any behaviour that disrupts the management of such a mission. Such a focus is quite technicist, with little need for distractions like critical analysis—philosophical or otherwise. For teachers or students to question such policy is easily and usually construed as negative or cynical resistance, detracting from their effectiveness in achieving desired outcomes.

Proud of its achievements, the New Zealand Ministry of Education (2010a) website specifies some 'ongoing initiatives' spanning early childhood, primary, intermediate and secondary education. These initiatives are 'designed to produce a high-income, knowledge-based economy that includes all New Zealanders'. Current initiatives focus sector-wide on truancy, pastoral care, professional development, raising achievement, personalized learning and collaboration between agencies.

This list of such initiatives is rather limited, technicist rather than philosophical in nature, and clearly designed to support an agenda of economic productivity. There is a focus on strengthening student achievement, and on the promotion of national standards in literacy and numeracy (reading, writing and mathematics), by being clear about what students should achieve and by when. There are national standards for Māori as well, and a focus on 'positive behaviour for learning'. Significant space is also dedicated to the National Digital Strategy and ensuring that schools are ready for ultra-fast broadband when it becomes available. No philosophy, though.

National Standards for Children

National Standards have been implemented in primary and intermediate schools across New Zealand this year. These are intended to rank all children above, below or well below, benchmarks in reading, writing and mathematics. Schools are to set achievement targets in their charters next year, and begin submitting data to the Ministry in 2012, on levels of achievement against those targets. There has been considerable resistance to the introduction of the new standards. One of the concerns is that the country is headed towards national league tables that rank schools according to assessment of the standards. The Principals' Federation is canvassing for money for an information campaign against the standards. The Auckland Primary Principals Association has already pledged $60,000 towards the campaign to put the Standards on hold.

Minister of Education Anne Tolley has called the resistance a 'silly political game', and criticized the Principals' Association for bringing 'nothing positive to the table': 'I can only conclude this is about egos, and nothing to do with lifting achievement for our children', Tolley is reported as saying (Hartevelt, 2010). The Minister also removed from the Parliament website a Parliamentary Library research paper released in June this year, although it subsequently appeared for a short time in the Google cache (R0B, 2010). Mrs Tolley said that the paper was 'unprofessional', 'highly political' and so biased 'it could have been written by the union opposing the policy' (Young, 2010). In the paper, research analyst Charlotte Oakley (2010) examines the introduction of the Standards, sympathetic to the view of the resistors—in terms of schools having been given insufficient time and professional development to become familiar with the Standards, to develop effective moderation processes, or to trial the standards to determine whether they have been set at the correct level. She signals potential motivation problems for students who do not achieve the Standards, and argues that it is teaching and learning, rather than the Standards themselves, that raise achievement levels. This, she says, may not be adequately provided for under the Standards. Not much philosophy here, either.

... and for Teachers?

Hartevelt's newspaper article also reports Auckland University professor John Hattie as wanting a similar set of standards to apply to teachers, with a group of 'experts' in charge of monitoring them. His concern is that teachers are currently allowed to do 'anything they want, as long as it's not harmful' (Hartevelt, 2010). He is concerned about the failure of the Teachers Council to set minimum standards for teachers, despite having received about 1000 complaints about teacher behaviour and competency, and having deregistered over 100 teachers, banning them from the profession. Hattie supports minimum standards to keep undesirables out of the profession, but says it is just as important to focus on excellence and effective performance. Again, there is no philosophical discourse surrounding this issue, and Hattie is one of the chosen few in the Independent Advisory Group for National Standards to advise on aspects of the implementation of the National Standards policy (Ministry of Education, 2010b).

A Vision for the Teaching Profession

The Minister of Education's workforce advisory group recently released its report, *A vision for the teaching profession* (Ministry of Education, 2010c). It provides a prescriptive focus on various aspects of teaching, including initial teacher education, supporting new teachers, career paths and leadership development. What stands out in the report is the reductionist focus on teachers' *skills* and *abilities*, a heavy reliance on *standards*, and a sense of locking down the controls on the profession. There is to be 'strengthened initial teacher education' (p. 5), 'compulsory training and development' for principals (p. 8) and 'robust standards throughout the profession' (p. 15). In true managerialist fashion, there are to be 'high standards of excellence' (p. 7), 'profession-wide recognition of excellence' (p. 16) and 'flexibility for school leaders to reward effective teachers' (p. 15).

Despite the group's recommendation that professional leadership must be 'owned by the profession and distinct from government or industrial bodies' (p. 2), the report advocates 'strengthening the capability and capacity of the New Zealand Teachers Council to take ownership and responsibility for: ... ethical accountability of teacher and discipline' (p. 17). There are two noteworthy concerns here: first, the Teachers Council is very much a government-controlled body; and secondly, this mention of ethics stems from a concern that 'there are no comprehensive and binding ethical standards required of teachers' (p. 24). One could, at a stretch, claim that we are talking philosophy when we mention ethics, but what is signified is actually compulsory compliance with pre-established rules. No philosophy, then, in the prescribed vision for the teaching profession.

Managing Disruptive Behaviour

Of growing significance in the education policy arena over recent years is a focus on the management of undesirable behaviour. An ongoing group of so-called experts, the Advisory Group on Conduct Problems (AGCP), provides advice to the Government about the development of programmes and policies to address conduct problems in childhood. The group has now published its second report on the prevention, treatment and management of conduct problems in young people (AGCP, 2009). The focus of this report is on the identification, implementation and evaluation of programmes and interventions for children aged 3–7. The gaze of the advisory group is strongly on psychological, psychiatric and therapeutic programmes as a backing for the authority of regular institutional discipline (school and family). The group recommend close alignment with a 'prevention science paradigm' (AGCP, 2009, p. 9), i.e. an approach based on evidence from the scientific literature, preceded by a pilot research programme, featuring randomized controlled trials, and implementing programmes on a population-wide basis across the entire country. Desirable outcomes of the group's preferred programmes include encouraging parents to seek help and to destigmatize treatment seeking, and a reduction in antisocial and problem behaviours in children in both the home and the school.

A similar behaviour management focus is evident in the Positive Behaviour for Learning Action Plan which, despite the 'positive' spin, is clearly billed as a mechanism for the 'management of disruptive behaviour in the education system' (New Zealand Government, 2009). Not much philosophy here, either, especially not of the troublesome kind.

Towards Uniformity

This brief overview of a few policy initiatives signals the current direction for education: increasingly standardized as a commodity, pluralism and diversity stifled, and student behaviour normalized under a strongly regulatory regime. Taken together, we see a convergence among the policies, the programmes and the agencies that deliver them; a convergence structured by, guided by and increasingly provided by those Jacques Donzelot (1979) called the 'psy' specialists and their apologists in education.[2] Advisory committees for such programmes draw heavily for their composition, their findings and their recommendations on proponents of psychology and psychiatry, so there is little interrogation of the terms of reference for such committees and even less criticism of the political agenda of those responsible for establishing such committees in the first place. The increasing 'psy' focus in education promotes the kind of discipline that Foucault identified in his genealogy of prison practices, through which objective classifications are adopted and accepted, certain knowledge and behaviours normalized, and particular individual identities constructed—the production of what he called 'docile bodies':

> not only so that they may do what one wishes, but so that they may operate as one wishes, with the techniques, the speed and the efficiency that one determines. Thus discipline produces subjected and practised bodies, 'docile' bodies. (Foucault, 1977, p. 138)

Philosophy has a war on its hands if it is to critically investigate the policy world or introduce an ethical dimension to educational dialogue. Something called 'philosophy' might appear within the walls of our educational institutions, but only if it does not challenge the *status quo*. As indicated at the outset of this article, philosophy is a complex domain, even within the restricted focus of this article. To explore a little further, I want to look at two perspectives on philosophy in relation to school: the first posits philosophy as a set of reasoned, reasonable and probably acceptable activities within the school community; the second questions the very structure of that community, and is not likely to be so warmly welcomed. As labels for such perspectives, we might call the first *harmless*, the second *dangerous*.

Philosophy as Harmless

Much has been argued about whether philosophy is the domain of a small group of experts, or whether the uninitiated might usefully participate actively and constructively in the discussing philosophical issues of current concern (e.g. Long, 2005). There are further issues about whether philosophy should be studied for its own sake, or treated more instrumentally as a kind of intellectual tool, to sharpen thinking skills. Both aspects are evident in the Matthew Lipman's (1976) rationale for promoting Philosophy for Children (P4C), although his major focus seems to be that it would improve reasoning (Lipman, 1976).

Although various initiatives have involved children in philosophy over the years, Lipman is credited with having developed philosophy for children as a commercial brand (Cohen & Naylor, 2008). His concern was for the teaching of reasoning in a way that might counteract the negative effects of school, nurturing within the classroom the 'lively curiosity that seems to be an essential part of the child's natural impulse' (Lipman, 1976, p. 22). For Lipman, the greatest disappointment of traditional education was its failure to produce people approximating his ideal of reasonableness.

Acknowledging the range of programmes around the world that bring philosophy and children together, Reed and Johnson (2000) see something unique about P4C programmes: the notion of the educated person as one who can think for herself or himself, along with a general methodology for nurturing that educated person. The same authors suggest that the assumption behind P4C is that getting children to *talk well* is a major step in creating a person who can 'think well for herself or himself' (p. 206). By talking well, they mean listening to each other, correcting others and themselves, being sensitive to the nuances of conversation, and searching for appropriate rules and standards for deciding what to say. In terms of general methodology, one starts from a specifically chosen text that is philosophically rich and interesting, with children's responses to the text forming the agenda for inquiry. Discussions evolve from the children's interests, and it is up to the teacher to seize upon these opportunities and use them as entries into philosophical exploration:

> getting as many views on out the table as there are children in the class-room, exposing the children to additional views that have been thought up by philosophers, examining the consequences of holding one view over another, and clarifying the meaning and tune underlying assumptions of each view. (Lipman, 1977/2000, p. 225)

Significant among the characteristics of P4C, as explained by Lipman, is the teacher's role as 'a fosterer of inquiry, a facilitator of dialogue, a guarantor of impartiality and an instigator of thinking for oneself' (Lipman, 1994/2000, p. 211). The classroom becomes a 'community of inquiry', with a broader vision of such communities nested within larger communities, and these within larger communities still. The image is an outward ripple effect, with 'individuals committed to self-corrective exploration and creativity' (Lipman, 1988/2000, p. 220).

Lipman identifies both a narrower and a broader case for P4C. The narrower case is simply that it makes a 'wholesome contribution to the present curriculum and the classroom', whereas the broader justification is a 'heuristic praxis of shared philosophical inquiry' (1988/2000, p. 216). The narrower case is conceded without argument, and can readily be subsumed within existing school pedagogy. It is this second and broader justification with which I am more concerned, particularly the limits to what might be examined in this 'heuristic praxis'. Experiential learning implies some engagement with experience. Where classrooms (and here I include the university environment) have been sanitized and insulated from the political context of education, exploration and investigation is limited. Lipman differentiates between the 'tribal' model of education, in which the child is initiated into a culture, and the 'reflective' model, which generates a certain subjective distance from that cultural environment. The first provides for the 'assimilation of the child by the culture', whereas the second provides for the 'appropriation of the culture by the child' (Lipman, 1988/2000, p. 220). To practise philosophy in ways that leave untouched the cultural and political milieu in which schooling practices and education policy are embedded seems to me very much the assimilation of the child by the culture.

Lipman talks further about philosophy as 'the mother of all sciences', generating new ideas in the speculative activity that precedes scientific understandings in new fields of knowledge:

> As philosophical speculation becomes more rigorous and substantiated, as measurement and experimentation and verification begin to occur, philosophy turns into science. In this sense, philosophy is a source of ideas that precedes the development of every new scientific enterprise. (Lipman, 1977/2000, pp. 224–225)

Philosophy is, he suggests, the discipline that best prepares us to think in terms of the other disciplines, and so must be assigned a central role in the educational process. Philosophers are, he says, 'critics of thinking' (1994/2000, p. 211) in much the same way that drama critics are critics of plays and political commentators are critics of policies. It is this role as critics of thinking that I want to amplify here. 'Thinking' does not occur in a vacuum; it involves thinking about something. In the case of education, it is acceptable to reflect on various forms of pedagogy, on classroom interactions, on the ways in which prescribed curricula can be rearranged and learning accelerated. It is less acceptable to think about the global political environment in which such curricula are prescribed, or to investigate the pendulum swings in prescribed curriculum and preferred pedagogy that accompany the changing agendas of various governments. What is clearly lacking in 'thinking about education', and equally lacking in the critics of such thinking, i.e. the philosophers, is the rigorous, reasoned analysis of the political backdrop for education policy, the commitment to exposing the ways in which universities are fast relinquishing their role as critic and conscience of society, and the exposition of the way that educational discourse is becoming lopsided, with psychology as the yardstick for education and the 'psy' specialists normalized as the arbiter for all things educational—even the category 'normal' itself.

There is much in P4C that would seem familiar to classroom teachers since the days of Dewey. It emphasizes the relationship between meaningful education and children's experience, it values Socratic dialogue and their participation in the educational relationship, while not losing sight of knowledge traditions. I recognize from my own days as a classroom teacher many approaches that were an everyday part of subjects such as science, language and social studies, where children were hypothesizing, working in groups to justify their thinking, engaging in intentional lateral thinking, etc. So, at the level of developing thinking, and even reflecting on the thinking process itself, P4C looks pretty much like business as usual, with some concessions made for the deliberate introduction of traditional philosophical concepts.

Before I let Lipman go, I want to draw upon one more observation of his. Philosophy is a survivor, he says, in an era in which most of the humanities have been driven to the wall. But, he acknowledges, the price of survival has been high: it has survived largely by converting itself into a knowledge industry. Philosophy has had to 'abdicate virtually all claims to exercising a socially significant role', contributing to what he calls 'the continued social impotence of philosophy' (Lipman, 1988/2000, p. 212). I am not objecting here to the principles underpinning P4C, or any other philosophy programme for that matter, as there is clearly much of value therein. I do see, though, that in its retreat to the safety of its cave, philosophy is currently shirking its duty in some areas of thinking, and particularly the thinking that needs to be done about the broader social and political issues in education.

Philosophy as Dangerous

I want to suggest another possible role for philosophy in schools, in terms of Maxine Greene's 'education for freedom', and the somewhat more radical Friedrich Nietzsche's 'philosopher of the future'. Both represent a challenge to philosophy and an invitation to extend its meticulous gaze beyond the immediate pedagogical environment, to probe the less visible (but thereby, more insidious) influences that shape both the official curriculum and broader societal agenda for its educational institutions.

Maxine Greene

Although her focus is on American schools, there is little in Greene's analysis that is uniquely American. She refers to the passivity and disinterest that prevent discoveries in classrooms and discourage inquiries, reminiscent of Dewey's notion of the 'anaesthetic' in experience, as what numbs people and prevents them from reaching out, from launching inquiries. It is not, she says, simply a matter of motivation or interest; but, rather, a problem with the absence of freedom in our schools. This is not just a reference to the ordinary limits and constraints, or even the rules established to ensure order. She is talking about the apparent absence of concern for the ways in which young people are conditioned by their circumstances—a form of cultural reproduction, involving 'not only the reproduction of ways of knowing, believing, and valuing, but the maintenance of social patterings and stratifications as well' (Greene, 1988/2000, p. 132).

The challenge for educators, she says, is to 'engage as many young people as possible in the thought that is freedom' (Greene, 1988/2000, p. 133). Developing a concern for the critical and the imaginative, and opening up new ways of looking at things are, she contends, wholly at odds with the technicist and behaviourist emphasis in schools. The remedy is to be found not within the heavily subjugated structure of schooling, but in an external focus on the broader political spectrum:

> I do not think it sufficient to develop even the most variegated, most critical, most imaginative, most 'liberal' approach to the education of the young. If we are seriously interested in education for freedom as well as for

the opening of cognitive perspectives, it is also important to find a way of developing a praxis of educational consequence that opens the spaces necessary for the remaking of a democratic community. (Greene, 1988/2000, p. 134)

Such an opening would mean, says Greene, 'fresh and sometimes startling winds blowing through the classrooms of the nation' (1988/2000, p. 134). Our traditional modes of sense-making—the academic disciplines, the fields of study—all have a place as particular kinds of questions posed at particular moments in time. But none of them should be considered complete or all-encompassing. In the multiple worlds our young people inhabit, new languages are needed to deal with the new undercurrents, the new questions, the new uncertainties. As educators, our role is to grant audibility to these numerous and different voices in an attitude of mutuality and responsiveness to others, struggling alongside our students as subjects in search of their own projects, their own ways of making sense of the world. We are in the realm here of what Nel Noddings (1994) describes as *care*, as we step out of one's own personal frame of reference into the others': 'When we care, we consider the other's point of view, his objective needs, and what he expects of us. Our attention, our mental engrossment, is on the cared-for, not on ourselves' (p. 24).

Rational argument falls somewhat short of the task in hand, as we face the issue of incommensurability, in search of critiques that uncover what masquerade as neutral frameworks, hat Rorty calls, 'a set of rules which will tell us how rational agreement can be reached on what would settle the issue on every point where statements seem to conflict' (Rorty, 1979, p. 316). Amid such multiplicity and with an attitude of inquiry and care for the other, philosophy has the capacity to redefine the territory of education and to challenge the political frameworks that blinker both teachers and students alike. Without the assurance of commensurability, without the promise of any final answers, teachers and students are left with questions, with tentative modes of inquiry, with multiple stories, and with the possibility of 'communities grounded in trust, flowering by means of dialogue, kept alive in open spaces where freedom can find a place' (Greene, 1988/2000, p. 140). Greene says that windows have to be opened in schools to let in the fresh air of aesthetic imagination, while for Noddings it is the happiness of actively responding to others. Not traditional philosophy, but open and holistic.

Nietzsche

With the windows wide open, it is refreshing to recall the work of Friedrich Nietzsche, a self-professed 'philosopher of the future' (Nietzsche, 1886/1990a, p. 71), for whom the philosophical task is manifest in his image of the 'free spirit', positioned uncomfortably outside the prevailing mores, prepared to challenge the *status quo*, and so destined for a life of solitude:

> It seems to me more and more that the philosopher, being *necessarily* a man of tomorrow and the day after tomorrow, has always found himself and *had* to find himself in contradiction to his today: his enemy has always been the

ideal of today. Hitherto these extraordinary promoters of mankind who have been called philosophers and have seldom felt themselves to be friends of knowledge but, rather, disagreeable fools and dangerous question marks—have found their task, their hard, unwanted, unavoidable task, but finally the greatness of their task, in being the a bad conscience of their age. (Nietzsche, 1886/1990a, p. 143)

There is little in Nietzsche's work as hard hitting as his lifelong commitment to the interrogation of truth. His own foreword to *Twilight of the idols* positions the book as 'a grand declaration of war' on eternal idols (Nietzsche, 1888/1990b, p. 32). Subtitled *How to philosophize with a hammer*, it easily evokes images of destruction and demolition. Yet, Nietzsche is careful to point out that the idols are being 'touched with the hammer as with a tuning fork'. He was to clarify some years later that what he refers to as *idol* was 'simply what has been called truth so far. *Twilight of the Idols*—that is, the old truth is approaching its end' (Nietzsche, 1887/1989, p. 314). There have been, he says, 'no more ancient idols in existence' and also 'none more hollow', but that does not prevent their 'being the *most believed in*', although 'they are not, especially in the most eminent case, called idols' (Nietzsche, 1888/1990b, p. 32). In typical colourful style, and amplifying his triumph over what has been called truth so far, Nietzsche goes on: '... to pose questions with a hammer and perhaps to receive for answer that famous hollow sound which speaks of inflated bowels ... that which would like to stay silent *has to become audible*' (Nietzsche, 1888/1990b, p. 31)

For Nietzsche, such challenges typify the free spirits who are the 'actual philosophers', the commanders and law-givers. It is they who determine the 'Wherefore and Whither of mankind', reaching for the future with a creative hand ... 'everything that is or has been becomes for them a means, an instrument, a hammer' (Nietzsche, 1886/1990a, p. 143). Nietzsche is quick to contrast his figure of the actual philosopher with what he calls 'philosophical labourers' like Kant and Hegel, whose work constitutes taking existing creations of value (sometimes called 'truths'), identifying them and reducing them to formulae: 'It is the duty of these scholars to take everything that has hitherto happened and been valued, and make it clear, distinct, intelligible and manageable, to abbreviate everything long, even "time" itself, and to *subdue* the entire past' (Nietzsche, 1886/1990a, p. 142). Far from providing the open window and the fresh air alluded to earlier, these philosophical labourers are portrayed as a 'narrow, enclosed, chained up species of spirits ... closed windows and bolted doors ... eloquent and tirelessly scribbling slaves of the democratic taste and its "modern ideas"' (Nietzsche, 1886/1990a, p. 72).

Nietzsche's opposition to his 'philosophical labourers' runs deep, with criticism directed at their glorification of the abstract, at their lack of historical sense, and at their denial of the senses in favour of abstract reason. We perceive the world, says Nietzsche, in terms of plurality, change and becoming, whereas *their* preference is for a world of unity, of substance and duration—a preference underpinned by abstract reason. Reason, Nietzsche says, is the cause of our falsification of the evidence of the senses. In so far as the senses show becoming, passing away, change, they do not lie: 'It is what we make of their evidence that first introduces a lie into it, for example the lie of unity, the lie of materiality, of substance, of duration' (Nietzsche, 1888/1990b, p. 46).

> They think they are doing a thing *honour* when they dehistoricize it ... when they make a mummy of it. All that philosophers have handled for millennia has been conceptual mummies; nothing actual has escaped from their hands alive. They kill, they stuff, when they worship, these conceptual idolaters—they come a mortal danger to everything when they worship. (Nietzsche, 1888/1990b, p. 45)

These false philosophers pose as having made their discoveries through the 'self-evolution of a cold, pure, divinely unperturbed dialectic', whereas what happens at bottom, Nietzsche claims, is that they are merely defending a prejudice, a notion, an 'inspiration', generally a desire of the heart sifted and made abstract, with reasons sought after the event. They are then, no better than 'cunning pleaders for their prejudices, which they baptize *truths*' (Nietzsche, 1886/1990a, p. 36).

He sees that philosophy under the yoke of the university (for our purposes, read 'schools') has no dignity or fire, and is no longer 'dangerous'. At the conclusion of his essay on Schopenhauer, Nietzsche makes a final plea for the importance of philosophy and its need to be powerful and fearsome:

> 'Beware', says Emerson, 'when the great God lets loose a thinker on this planet. Then all things are at risk.' It is as when a conflagration has broken out in a great city, and no man knows what is safe, or where it will end. (Nietzsche, 1874/1983, p. 193)

And, stepping up to the mark, donning the mantle of the dangerous philosopher:

> I know my fate. One day my name will be associated with the memory of something tremendous—a crisis without equal on earth, the most profound collision of conscience, a decision that was conjured up *against* everything that had been believed, demanded, hallowed so far. I am no man, I am dynamite. (Nietzsche, 1887/1989, p. 326)

Conclusion

Philosophy and schools? Children and dynamite? Hardly the easiest of bedfellows! So, in considering the relationship between philosophy and schools, I am left with two answers.

What I have called harmless philosophy may have an explicit place in schools, supporting a conservative agenda, sharpening up reasoning ability and promoting thinking about abstract thinking. Such engagement is likely to leave existing educational frameworks intact, traditional classroom programmes and interactions valid, and the purposes of schools unquestioned, as long as one ignores disruptive behaviour. There is room for philosophy in schools: Plato's cave remains undisturbed.

Philosophy of the dangerous kind, though, is a different matter. To the degree that it is abhorrent to schools, it is probably needed. If schools are to go beyond their current functioning as government-directed networks of social and cultural subjectivity, then philosophy needs to exercise its critical faculties. Troublesome possibilities then arise for political, conceptual and social transformation. Commitment to critical philosophy becomes, then, a flexing of political muscle: a necessarily surreptitious activity on the part of individual teachers, operating outside the official curriculum and frustrated by increasing surveillance and demand for accountability. Philosophy of the dangerous kind is, then, a commitment not so much to philosophy *in* schools, as to philosophy *over* schools.

Notes

1. Compulsory attendance is monitored in terms of truancy and disciplinary measures such as stand-downs, suspensions, exclusions and expulsions—this lot under the guise of student presence and engagement (Ministry of Education, 2007).
2. Donzelot includes in this group those practising psychology, psychiatry, psychotherapy and psycho-pedagogy. The 'psy' specialists are charged with shaping subjectivity at the intersection of society and family (Donzelot, 1997, pp. 229–230).

References

AGCP [Advisory Group on Conduct Problems]. (2009, November). *Conduct problems: Effective programmes for 3–7 year-olds*. Retrieved December 16, 2009, from http://www. moh.govt.nz/moh.nsf/pagesmh/9995/$File/conduct-problems-effective-programmes-for-3-7-year-olds.pdf

Cohen, M., & Naylor, L. (2008). Philosophy in schools. *The Philosopher, LXXXXVI*(1). Retrieved September 12, 2010, from http://www.the-philosopher.co.uk/p4cgallions.htm

Donzelot, J. (1979). *The policing of families*. New York: Pantheon.

Foucault, M. (1977). *Discipline and punish* (A. Sheridan, Trans.). London: Penguin.

Greene, M. (2000). The dialectic of freedom. In R. Reed & T. Johnson (Eds.), *Philosophical documents in education* (pp. 123–141). New York: Addison-Wesley Longman. (Original work published 1988).

Hartevelt, J. (2010, August 29). Tolley hits at 'silly political game'. *Sunday Star Times*, p. 7.

Lipman, M. (1976). Philosophy for Children. *Metaphilosophy, 7*, 17–33.

Lipman, M. (2000). Philosophy in the classroom. In R. Reed & T. Johnson (Eds.), *Philosophical documents in education* (pp. 221–225). New York: Addison-Wesley Longman. (Original work published 1977).

Lipman, M. (2000). Philosophy goes to school. In R. Reed & T. Johnson (Eds.), *Philosophical documents in education* (pp. 212–221). New York: Addison-Wesley Longman. (Original work published 1988).

Lipman, M. (2000). Do elementary school children need philosophy? In R. Reed & T. Johnson (Eds.), *Philosophical documents in education* (pp. 207–212). New York: Addison-Wesley Longman. (Original work published 1994).

Long, F. (2005). Thomas Reid and philosophy with children. *Journal of Philosophy of Education, 39*, 599–614.

Ministry of Education. (2007). *Statement of intent 2007–2012*. Wellington: Ministry of Education.

Ministry of Education. (2010a, June 4). *Education initiatives*. Retrieved September 8, 2010, from http://www.minedu.govt.nz/theMinistry/EducationInitiatives.aspx

Ministry of Education. (2010b, March 24). *Terms of reference—Independent Advisory Group for National Standards*. Retrieved September 16, 2010, from http://www.minedu.govt.nz/the-Ministry/EducationInitiatives/NationalStandards/TOR.aspx

Ministry of Education. (2010c, April). *A vision for the teaching profession: Education Workforce Advisory Group report to the Minister of Education*. Retrieved June 10, 2010, 2010, from http://www.minedu.govt.nz/~/media/MinEdu/Files/TheMinistry/Consultation/WorkforceAdvisoryGroup/WorkforceAdvisoryGroupFinalReportPDF.pdf

New Zealand Government. (2009, December 7). *Positive Behaviour for Learning Action Plan 2010–2014*. Retrieved December 16, 2009, from http://www.minedu.govt.nz/~/media/MinEdu/Files/TheMinistry/PositiveBehaviourForLearning/PositiveBehaviouForLearningActionPlan.pdf

Nietzsche, F. (1983). Schopenhauer as educator. In C. Taylor (Ed.), *Untimely meditations* (pp. 125–194). Cambridge: Cambridge University Press. (Original work published 1874).

Nietzsche, F. (1989). *On the genealogy of morals and Ecce homo* (W. Kaufmann, Trans.). New York: Vintage. (Original work published 1887).

Nietzsche, F. (1990a). *Beyond good and evil* (R. Hollingdale, Trans.). London: Penguin. (Original work published 1886).

Nietzsche, F. (1990b). *Twilight of the idols & The anti-christ* (R. J. Hollingdale, Trans.). London: Penguin. (Original work published 1888).

Noddings, N. (1984). *Caring: A feminine approach to ethics and moral education*. Berkeley, CA: University of California Press.

Oakley, C. (2010). *National Standards (research paper 2010/03)*. Retrieved July 7, 2010, from http://webcache.googleusercontent.com/search?q=cache:nAkAgT_0TrkJ:www.parliament.nz/en-NZ/ParlSupport/ResearchPapers/

Quinton, A. (1995). Philosophy. In T. Honderich (Ed.), *The Oxford companion to philosophy* (pp. 666–670). Oxford: Oxford University Press.

R0B. (2010, June 30). *The paper that Anne Tolley censored*. Retrieved September 16, 2010, from http://thestandard.org.nz/the-paper-that-anne-tolley-censored/

Reed, R., & Johnson, T. (2000). Introduction. In R. Reed & T. Johnson (Eds.), *Philosophical documents in education* (pp. 204–207). New York: Addison-Wesley Longman.

Rorty, R. (1979). *Philosophy and the mirror of nature*. Princeton, NJ: Princeton University Press.

Young, A. (2010, June 30). Tolley upset at paper on standards. *New Zealand Herald*.

Opening Teachers' Minds to Philosophy: The crucial role of teacher education

SUE KNIGHT & CAROL COLLINS

School of Education, University of South Australia

Abstract

Why has the 'Philosophy for Children' movement failed to make significant educational inroads in Australia, given the commitment and ongoing efforts of philosophers and educators alike who have worked hard in recent decades to bring philosophy to our schools? In this article we single out one factor as having particular importance, namely, that, on the whole, teachers consider philosophical inquiry to be futile. We argue that the explanation rests with teachers' underlying epistemological beliefs and that openness to philosophy depends upon teachers being disposed to engage in the practices of reason-giving and reason evaluation, being aware of the epistemic value of such practices and, concomitantly, having highly developed reasoning skills. Drawing on both anecdotal evidence and wide-ranging research from within cognitive psychology, we go on to make a case for change within teacher education programmes.

Introduction: Where is Philosophy for Children Now?

There was cause for optimism when professional teacher associations responsible for promoting Philosophy for Children (P4C) in Australian schools formed a national coordinating body called FAPCA in 1989. The situation at the time of writing this article (2010), then, can only be seen as a vast disappointment. Although those working with P4C have exerted some influence on state-wide and national-level curriculum frameworks and succeeded in creating a small number of flagship schools, the P4C movement has failed to make significant educational inroads in Australia.[1] While the 'Educational Goals for Young Australians' describes successful learners as (in part) '... able to think deeply and logically, and obtain and evaluate evidence in a disciplined way ...' (Ministerial Council on Education, Employment, Training, and Youth Affairs, 2008, pp. 8–9), no state or territory education department sets aside a dedicated place in the curriculum for the development of these skills and dispositions. The proposed National Curriculum for Australian Schools, like the state curriculum frameworks, identifies these capabilities as educationally important, yet again would appear to stop short of specifying philosophy as the vehicle through which to develop such abilities. Moreover, few, if any, Australian teacher education programmes have P4C as a core curriculum course; the $30 million National Values Education programme and the equally well-funded Discovering Democracy programme were developed in the absence of input from P4C advocates and are altogether devoid of philosophical content.[2] This is a bitter pill to swallow for those who, for over 25 years, have continued to work to support teachers and to promote philosophy in schools. The singular benefits of philosophy continue to be appreciated by the tiny minority of educators who have studied the subject at university level, by again, a small minority of teachers, perhaps because they have managed to retain a child-like curiosity about the world or perhaps because, in philosophical thinking, they recognize a rigour and depth characteristic of good thinking. But for every one such teacher there are 100 more who turn instead to de Bono's creative thinking exercises or his 'Six Hats' programme or, authoritatively, to the list of ten 'Common Values for Australian Schools'.[3]

The explanation would appear to involve a complex array of factors. Ideologically, there is a continuing reliance on Piagetian and Kohlbergian developmental stage theories, according to which young children are not yet capable of abstract thinking, and therefore not able to participate in philosophical reasoning (Duska & Whelan, 1977). Available research provides ample evidence of young children's philosophical capabilities (Lipman & Gazzard, 1988; Trickey & Topping, 2004; García-Moriyón, Rebolllo, & Colom, 2005; Collins, 2005; Lyle, 2008) and suggests that philosophy has not been taken up widely in schools owing to a prejudice that attempts to answer philosophical questions will lead to indoctrination, that asking controversial questions may offend some students, their parents or the school administration. More pragmatic concerns are the crowded curriculum and, on the part of teachers, a lack of the knowledge and skills required to engage children in philosophical discussion (Collins, 2005). It seems plausible to suggest that all these factors, and probably others, are influential in restricting the uptake of philosophy for children. In this article we argue that the fundamental factor underpinning these reasons is that on the whole, teachers consider philosophical inquiry to be futile.

Our evidence is in part anecdotal, garnered from countless interactions with teachers and pre-service teachers. Although, like others across Australia, we are fortunate to have been involved with several local primary school communities in which philosophy has been implemented successfully and thrived for many years, we have also witnessed, all too often, teachers displaying a distaste for philosophical inquiry. For example, we have been invited, on numerous occasions, to provide whole-staff professional development workshops aimed at introducing the P4C programme to primary teachers and supporting these teachers to develop the requisite skills to facilitate philosophical inquiry discussions with their students. The invitations are usually extended by principals keen to tap into the potential benefits philosophy may bring their students and the wider school community. Invariably, however, many among the staff seem resistant, and at times even hostile, to the prospect of a new school focus on philosophy and the possibility that they may be required to draw philosophical inquiry into their own teaching practice. Many teachers, working in an overcrowded curriculum, express their frustration at losing precious teaching and learning time to discussing abstract ideas that are seemingly irrelevant to the concerns of the mainstream curriculum.

Similarly, during professional development workshops designed to encourage teachers to think through and discuss relevant philosophical issues, their frustration often appears to be compounded by a perception that there is little or no point in raising philosophical questions with children, or perhaps with anyone, because such questions have no answers, or at least that it cannot be shown that any one answer is any better than another. Such a view among primary school teachers is also consistently reported by highly skilled and dedicated colleagues working to bring philosophy alive in their classrooms, with or without support from others in their school communities, and by student teachers attempting to include philosophical inquiry questions and discussion-based lessons in their practicum teaching experiences. Two local empirical studies (Collins, 1998; Lucas, 2000) lend direct support to such claims, reporting that when presented with a list of age-appropriate philosophical questions, only a tiny minority (12%) of primary school teachers indicated that they were likely to consider raising and discussing them with students.[4]

An Explanation: Teachers' Underlying Epistemic Beliefs

We contend that the explanation rests with teachers' underlying epistemological beliefs. Philosophical inquiry depends more on reasoning than it does on empirical research, although the latter also plays an important role. A willingness to engage in philosophical inquiry depends upon a disposition to look for and furnish reasons; an underlying epistemological approach, which, within cognitive psychology, is described as 'evaluativism'. The term comes out of a substantial body of research known as the Epistemological Levels research programme, and is taken to describe an underlying epistemological orientation; a disposition to employ a particular set of procedures in the attempt to justify one's beliefs (Knight & Collins, 2006). Researchers within this programme argue that an individual's view of what counts as adequate justification for, say, ethical or scientific beliefs, changes over time, and that what is more, these changes form a common developmental sequence (Kuhn, 1992; King & Kitchener, 1994). There is also recognition within the theory that an individual's epistemic stance may vary across knowledge domains, crucially, across the broad domains of physical science, social science and morality.[5]

Typically, structured interviews have been used to identify three broad stages of approaches to justification; three levels of epistemological development. The earliest stage has knowledge as simple, consisting of relatively unconnected facts, certain and absolute; handed down from authority, where the authority might take the form of an ideology, the mores of society, the dictates of an individual, or one's own or another's experience; experience which is held to speak for itself. Everyday examples of this approach include: 'Homosexuality is morally wrong because the Church forbids it'; 'Killing animals for food is morally right because it is part of our way of life'; 'The theory of evolution is false because it contradicts the Bible'. Mere appeal to authority is an inadequate and dangerous justificatory approach. The social dangers of blind adherence to business codes of conduct are all too obvious.

The second epistemological stage sees individuals aware not only that the views of different authorities can contradict one another, but that a particular authority's earlier views may well conflict with that same authority's later pronouncements. Beliefs are then held to take on the status of personal possessions to which each individual is entitled. The result is that all views are taken to have equal legitimacy and one's own view may be as reliable as that of an authority. At this stage individuals take the very act of holding a belief as justification for that belief; in other words, justification is held to be impossible, and therefore, logically, cannot be required. Philosophers have agreed that this, the relativist position, is untenable; generally accepting that the judicious use of evidence and reason provides grounds for the comparison of conflicting viewpoints.[6] It is clear, too, that relativism is dangerous, whether in science (over the issue, say, of global warming) or ethics (in relation to child slavery or female genital mutilation).

Evaluativism is the third epistemological stage, and is identified as the epistemic endpoint. An individual operating at this epistemic level is held to understand that conflicting viewpoints (on global warming, say, or female circumcision) can be compared and evaluated on the basis of reason and empirical evidence. They acknowledge the possibility of genuine interchange with those who hold conflicting opinions, and the possibility that they themselves might come to modify their views on the basis of rational argument. In other words, evaluativists are disposed to engage in the practices of reason-giving and reason evaluation *and* to see the epistemic value of such practices (Kuhn, 1992).

An evaluativist, then, when confronted with a philosophical question (say the metaphysical question, 'Do humans have free will?') will at least allow that the question is legitimate in that there are agreed upon processes of argument which, when employed judiciously, enable an inquirer to make progress towards an intersubjectively verifiable answer. For both absolutists and relativists, however, philosophical inquiry is futile.

One further finding from epistemological levels research is of interest here. Kuhn (1992) has shown a correlation between evaluativism and level of reasoning proficiency, measured in terms of the ability, when prompted, to provide genuine evidence for a theory (i.e. evidence which is both distinct from the theory and relevant to its correctness) and the ability to generate genuine counter-arguments and rebuttals. Unsurprisingly, it seems that the more one engages in the processes of reasoning the more skilled one's engagement becomes (Kuhn, 1992). Lipman made this connection between epistemological stance and proficiency in reasoning skills, suggesting that an individual with poorly developed reasoning skills is unlikely to appreciate the power of reasoning, the strength of the relevant truth procedures, so that when faced with a philosophical question is likely to retreat to an appeal-to-authority or relativist approach to justification. Conversely, he argues, highly developed reasoning skills make it possible for an individual to engage in fruitful philosophical inquiry, thereby coming to realize the justificatory value of the processes of argument (Lipman, 1985).

As noted earlier, an individual's epistemological stance is likely to vary across the broad domains of physical science, social science and morality, so that, for example, she might understand the strength of the truth procedures in physical science, while failing to recognize such truth procedures in morality. Evaluativism within a domain, then, must be tied to reasoning within that domain. It follows that a necessary condition for the adoption of an evaluativist stance across these three broad domains is immersion in the content area of each of those domains.[7] Such immersion is necessary though not sufficient: content knowledge can as easily result in an absolutist or a relativist epistemological stance as an evaluativist one. Meyer (2009), for example, found that tertiary students in the 'hard' disciplines (such as mathematics, chemistry and physics) tended to believe that knowledge in that discipline was certain, simple and obtained from authorities, while those in the 'soft' knowledge areas (such as psychology, history and education) viewed knowledge in these areas as complex, tentative and socially constructed.[8]

Whether or not we accept the linear developmental model of the cognitive psychologists, it would seem to follow that where teachers adopt either absolutist or relativist approaches to justification; where they see no epistemic value in looking for and furnishing reasons, and, as seems likely, also operate with underdeveloped reasoning skills, they are unlikely to be receptive to the idea of adding philosophy to the school curriculum. Openness to P4C would seem to depend upon teachers being disposed to engage in the practices of reason-giving and reason evaluation across knowledge domains, being aware of the epistemic value of such practices and, concomitantly, having highly developed reasoning skills, again across domains; in the psychologists' terms, thinking *consistently* as evaluativists.

Plausibility Considerations

We are suggesting, then, that P4C's lack of mainstream success in Australia can be explained, in part at least, in terms of teachers' underlying epistemological dispositions. At first sight this may seem unlikely. After all, Australian teacher registration is conditional upon completion of a four-year university degree. Most, if not all, Australian universities uniformly adopt sets of graduate outcomes which include the ability to think critically within a knowledge domain.[9] We might expect, then, that on the whole graduating teachers would understand the epistemic value of evaluativist practices, be disposed to employ these practices, and have developed the necessary reasoning skills to do so. Surely this is not an unrealistic expectation, given the length of teacher training degrees.

Yet epistemological levels research shows that the evaluativist stage is attained by only a small fraction of those students (Hofer & Pintrich, 2006). Ordinary degree students, even at the end of their programmes, appear to operate at absolutist or relativist levels (Kuhn, 1992; King & Kitchener, 1994). Moreover, a recent local study of the justificatory reasoning tendencies of final year undergraduate students across a broad range of degrees, including the Primary/Junior Primary Education degree, has shown that the majority of the participants exhibited absolutist and relativist tendencies in the moral and scientific domains (Meyer, 2009, p. 225). While this study did not test for reasoning skill proficiency, the well-established correlation, noted earlier, between epistemological level and reasoning proficiency would make it likely that the identified majority of final year students who employed absolutist and relativist modes of justification would also operate with poorly developed reasoning skills.

Over a decade ago, Richard Paul, Linda Elder, and Ted Bartell (1997) led a study of teacher education courses in 66 colleges and universities, in order to assess, '... the extent to which students in teacher preparation courses in California are being taught in ways that facilitate skill in critical thinking and the ability to teach it to others' (p. 2). Paul and colleagues use the term 'critical thinking' to refer to 'thinking that explicitly aims at well founded judgment and hence utilizes appropriate standards in the attempt to determine ... [truth]' (p. 2). This is what we have described as evaluativist thinking.

Information about how faculty members tend to think about critical thinking and the way in which their views influence their teaching was collected through in-depth interviews made up of both closed and open-ended questions. Among the quantitative findings were the following:

- Though the overwhelming majority (89%) claimed critical thinking to be a primary objective of their instruction, only a small minority (19%) could give a clear explanation of what critical thinking is. ... [An even smaller] minority could clearly explain the meanings of basic terms in critical thinking. For example, only 8% could clearly differentiate between an assumption and an inference, and only 4% could differentiate between an inference and an implication.
- When asked how they conceptualised truth, a surprising 41% of those who responded to the question said that knowledge, truth and sound judgement are fundamentally matters of personal preference or subjective taste. (Paul et al., 2001, pp. 3–4)

Paul and colleagues go on to report that:

> ... [A] significant percentage of faculty interviewed:
>
> - Do not consider reasoning as a significant focus of critical thinking
> - Cannot specify basic structures essential to the analysis of reasoning
> - Cannot give an intelligible explanation of basic abilities in ... critical thinking ...
> - Inadvertently confuse the active involvement of students in classroom activities with critical thinking in those activities. (Paul et al., 2001, pp. 3–4)

On the basis of these findings, they conclude:

> Careful analysis of the interviews indicates that ... most faculty have not carefully thought through any concept of critical thinking, have no sense of intellectual standards that they can put into words, and are, therefore by any reasonable interpretation, in no position to foster critical thinking in

their own students or to help them foster it in their future students—except to inculcate into their students the same vague views that they have. (Paul et al., 2001, p. 5).

While no comparable Australian studies have been undertaken, there is a number of sources of evidence to which we can appeal. As part of her 2009 study, Meyer carried out a comprehensive analysis of reports from recent inquiries into Australian teacher education,[10] finding in these reports no overt aim directed at the development of the skills and dispositions we have characterized as evaluativist thinking (Meyer, 2009). In addition, we can turn to findings from research into pedagogical practices that appear to be associated with the development of evaluativism. Two such practices stand out. The first is the explicit teaching of critical thinking skills, especially through the use of a mixed instructional approach which combines engagement in subject-related reasoning tasks with a separate stream designed to teach for a range of general reasoning skills and dispositions (Abrami et al., 2008). Secondly, we can point to engagement in collaborative, logically based discussion of ill-structured problems, sometimes referred to as *dialogic teaching* (Lyle, 2008). Very briefly, research from within cognitive psychology and the P4C movement over the past four decades demonstrates that engagement in such discussions enhances (among other things) individuals' epistemological development (Trickey & Topping, 2004; García-Moriyón et al., 2005; Collins, 2005; Lyle, 2008). Much of this research relates to a particular dialogic teaching approach known widely as the 'Community of Inquiry' (Splitter & Sharp, 1995; Lipman, 2003). In such forums attention is drawn to the procedures of critical thinking, as well as to the power of such procedures, so that both skills and epistemic understandings are fostered. Meyer (2009) also found that the community of inquiry approach and instruction in reason-giving and evaluation were both independently associated with an increase in pre-service teachers' tendency to engage in argument with others on controversial issues and a decrease in the tendency to avoid engaging in such argument.

We need to ask, then, to what extent these pedagogical practices have a place in current teacher education programmes in Australian universities. The question is hard to answer; a web-search is unlikely to reveal the detail we need. We do have some data, however, in Meyer's (2009) search of university web sites which revealed only six compulsory courses in teacher education programmes involving one or both of the identified practices. On this basis we conclude, tentatively, that not enough is being done in Australian teacher education courses to develop the skills and dispositions of evaluativism so that graduating teachers are unlikely to display openness to the idea of taking philosophy into their classrooms. Generalizing from Paul's findings, even where there are such courses, they are likely to stand alone in their advocacy for the skills and dispositions that make for evaluativist thinking. Worse, they might well be undermined by the epistemological approaches underlying other courses in the programme. As a result, their developmental effects are likely to be limited.

An Example

Within the University of South Australia's School of Education we teach two compulsory courses aimed at developing the skills and dispositions of evaluativism.

One of these courses, Society & Environment Education, aims to develop pre-service (junior primary/primary teachers') justificatory reasoning in the scientific and moral domains. Students are not only introduced to environmental and social science content and associated pedagogy, but also encouraged to appreciate the importance of making sound scientific and moral judgements about social and environmental issues (Knight & Collins, 2010b). We also introduce students to the dangers of absolutism and relativism.

In the second of our courses, Ethics, Education and Critical Inquiry, we begin by asking pre-service teachers to reflect on their goals as teachers and what they see as the purpose of education. We discuss the role that values play in teaching and look more closely at the elements of moral decision-making and the dangers of absolutism and relativism. We teach explicitly for the skills of logical cogency, including recognizing, furnishing and evaluating arguments, and demonstrate the power of deductively valid and inductively strong arguments. The course also includes a 'philosophy across the curriculum' component designed to demonstrate how unearthing the philosophical underpinnings of mathematics, science, technology, and so on, not only contributes to learning in those curriculum areas but also serves to develop reasoning skills and dispositions.[11] Importantly, both courses employ a dialogue-based community of inquiry approach and advocate this approach as the best method for developing evaluativist reasoning skills and dispositions in children. In addition, a new first year course designed to introduce students to big questions in science and mathematics will be characterized by a community of inquiry approach and an emphasis on truth procedures in these disciplines.

On a number of measures, including contribution to tutorial discussions, content of assignments and continued involvement in the South Australian Philosophy Teachers' Association, the courses appear to have made an impact on students' epistemological understandings and their openness to philosophical ideas and argument. In addition, Meyer's (2009) pre–post test intervention study showed that engagement in these two courses, '… was associated with significant increases in evaluativist reasoning tendencies and significant decreases in absolutist and relativist reasoning tendencies in all three domains [moral, physical science and social science]' (p. 236). Yet, we know that there is a significant proportion of students whose epistemological understandings remain unchanged and who leave their course believing, as they did when they entered it, that philosophical inquiry is futile.

Conclusion

If Philosophy for Children is ever to flourish in our primary schools, we need to do better. We urge philosophers of education to consider and act on the argument we have made for change within teacher education. For unless we are prepared to do more to open teachers' minds to philosophy, 25 years from now another writer might well be putting the same argument lamenting the general absence of philosophy in our classrooms.

Notes

1. We can point to Phil Cam's involvement in the development of Queensland's 'Productive Pedagogies', the introduction of senior secondary philosophy subjects in many Australian states including South Australia, Western Australia and Victoria, and Buranda State School's high profile as a philosophy-based school.
2. This situation is not restricted to Australia. At Montclair State University, the home of Philosophy for Children, the Institute for Advancement of Philosophy for Children is no longer supported by the university and has subsequently lost its director; the flagship journal *Thinking*, established by Mathew Lipman more than three decades ago, ceased publication in 2010, and elsewhere, teacher associations exert, a best, a sporadic influence, with fortunes dependent upon the energy and commitment of individual administrators, educators and academics. New Zealand and Scotland stand out as examples here.
3. See, for example, de Bono (1990) and the *Australian Values Education Framework*, available online: http://www.curriculum.edu.au/values/ (retrieved September 1, 2010).
4. The questions in these studies were ethical in nature and related to the topics of animal rights and contemporary indigenous issues. For example: 'Is it ok to eat eggs laid by battery hens?'; 'Should the Australian Government apologize to Aboriginal Australians?'
5. Kuhn, Cheney, and Weinstock (2000) explained such variation as demonstrating transition between epistemological levels.
6. See, for example, James R. Beebe's 'Moral relativism in context' (2010), on moral relativism. Relativism about science is disproved by the arguments behind the widely accepted theory of holism, stressing as it does the intersubjectivity of experience.
7. Recent research has indicated that an individual's epistemological stance can vary not only between domains, but within a single domain (Meyer, 2009). For example, a person might reason as an evaluativist in relation to Newtonian theories in physics, but appeal to religious authority in evaluating the truth of the theory of evolution. Such findings raise important questions in relation to education in both science and morals as well as in critical thinking. We would like to thank Alan Tapper for drawing our attention to this point.
8. Christopher Winch (2010) argues that the role of developing teachers' understandings of the epistemology of the subjects they teach lies with university Philosophy of Education courses.
9. As an example see the full list of the University of South Australia's Graduate Qualities and associated indicators; see: http://www.unisa.edu.au/gradquals/staff/indicators.asp (retrieved September 1, 2010).
10. See, for example, *The Future of Schooling in Australia* (2007), available online at education. qld.gov.au/publication/production/.../federalist-paper.pdf *(retrieved September 1, /2010)*; and *Teaching and Leading for Quality in Australian Schools* (2007), available at: http://www. aitsl.edu.au/ta/webdav/site/tasite/shared/Publications%20and%20Covers/Teaching%20and% 20Leading%20for%20Quality%20Australian%20Schools.pdf (retrieved September 1, 2010).
11. See our paper, 'Enlivening the curriculum: the power of philosophical inquiry', for a full discussion of the 'philosophy across the curriculum' approach (Knight & Collins, 2010a).

References

Abrami, P., Bernard, R., Borokhovski, E., Wade, A., Surkes, M., Tamin, R., & Zhang, D. (2008). Instructional interventions affecting critical thinking skills and dispositions: A stage one meta-analysis. *Review of Educational Research, 78*(4), 1102–1134.

Beebe, J. (2010). Moral relativism in context. *Nous, 44*(3), 1–34.

de Bono, E. (1990). *Six thinking hats*. London: Penguin.

Collins, C. (1998). *Philosophical inquiry in the classroom: Clearing the obstacles for teachers to build communities of inquiry. Hons. thesis*. Adelaide: University of South Australia.

Collins, C. (2005). Education for a just democracy: The role of ethical inquiry. PhD thesis, University of South Australia, Adelaide.

Duska, R., & Whelan, M. (1977). *Moral development: A guide to Piaget and Kohlberg*. Dublin: Gill and Macmillan.

García-Moriyón, F., Rebollo, I., & Colom, R. (2005). Evaluating Philosophy for Children: A meta-analysis. *Thinking, 17*(4), 14–22.

Hofer, B., & Pintrich, P. (1997). The development of epistemological theories: Beliefs about knowledge and knowing and their relation to learning. *Review of Educational Research, 67*(1), 88–140.

King, P., & Kitchener, K. (1994). *Developing reflective judgment: Understanding and promoting intellectual growth and critical thinking in adolescents and adults*. San Francisco, CA: Jossey-Bass.

Knight, S., & Collins, C. (2006). Cultivating reason-giving: The primary purpose of education? *International Journal of the Humanities, 3*(2), 187–194.

Knight, S., & Collins, C. (2010a). Enlivening the curriculum: The power of philosophical inquiry. *Theory and Research in Education, 8*(3), 305–318.

Knight, S., & Collins, C. (2010b). ETHIC: A procedure for ethical decision making within Society & Environment. *Social Educators' Association of Australia, Biennial Conference Proceedings*, Adelaide. Retrieved September 1, 2010, from http://www.seaa.org.au/adelaide2010.html

Kuhn, D. (1992). Thinking as argument. *Harvard Educational Review, 62*(2), 155–178.

Kuhn, D., Cheney, R., & Weinstock, M. (2000). The development of epistemological understandings. *Cognitive Development, 15*, 209–228.

Lipman, M. (1985). Philosophy and the cultivation of reasoning. *Thinking, 5*(4), 33–42.

Lipman, M. (2003). *Thinking in education* (2nd ed.). Cambridge: Press Syndicate of the University of Cambridge.

Lipman, M., & Gazzard, A. (1988). Philosophy for Children: Where are we now? *Thinking: The Journal of Philosophy for Thinking, 7*(4), Supplement 1, 1–12.

Lucas, J. (2000). *Aboriginal and Torres Strait Islander studies as an anti-racist strategy: Raising ethical questions. Hons. thesis*. Adelaide: University of South Australia.

Lyle, A. (2008). Dialogic teaching: Discussing theoretical contexts and reviewing evidence from classroom practice. *Language and Education, 22*(3), 222–240.

Meyer, T. (2009). Developing justificatory reasoning: The importance for teacher education. PhD thesis, University of South Australia, Adelaide.

Ministerial Council on Education, Employment, Training, and Youth Affairs. (2008). *The educational goals for young Australians*. Melbourne: Curriculum Corporation.

Paul, R., Elder, L., & Bartell, T. (2001). Executive summary: Study of 38 public universities and 28 public universities to determine faculty emphasis on critical thinking in instruction. Retrieved September 1, 2010, from http://www.criticalthinking.org/research/Abstract-RPAUL-38public.cfm

Splitter, L., & Sharp, A. (1995). *Teaching for better thinking: The classroom community of inquiry*. Melbourne: Australian Council for Educational Research.

Trickey, S., & Topping, K. (2004). Philosophy for Children. *Research Papers in Education, 19* (3), 365–380.

Winch, C. (2010). For philosophy of education in teacher education. *Philosophy of Education Society of Australasia Conference*, Perth, December 2010. http://www.pesa.org.au/site/page/conference.html

What is Philosophy for Children? From an educational experiment to experimental education

Nancy Vansieleghem

LUCA, Campus Sint-Lucas Visual Arts

Abstract

Philosophy seems to have gained solid ground in the hearts and minds of educational researchers and practitioners. We critique Philosophy for Children as an experimental programme aimed at improving children's thinking capacity, by questioning the concept of critique itself. What does it mean when an institutional framework like the school claims to question its own framework, and what is the consequence of such a claim for thinking, in education, philosophy and the child? Implications for the concept of critical thinking follow.

Introduction

Philosophy for Children (P4C) arose in the 1970s as an educational experiment and critique of traditional forms of education. It criticizes education for its institutional context and economic force that does not stimulate but obstructs thinking for oneself. With a growing demand for self-reflection and self-actualization in education, to what extent can a programme such as P4C still problematize society? What does it mean when an institutional framework like the school claims to question its own framework, and what is the consequence of such a claim for thinking, education, philosophy, critique and the child? When critical thinking becomes the central point of education, how can it offer a critique of the education system in which it is taught?

We are not arguing in favour of or against P4C. Rather, we will explore the kind of subject(ivity) that is generated through such an experimental programme. In line with Lyotard (1999), we suppose that critique no longer functions as an antithesis of the existing social order and power but that it has become a part of that order and power. We suppose that Lipman's critical experiment today can be described as an effect and an instrument of an advanced form of power (Lyotard, 1999; Masschelein, 2004). Power operates precisely through the intensification of critique; that the subject is addressed to think about himself or herself, the other and the world in order to be(come) free. This will lead us back to the question: what could P4C be about at a time in which critique has become an essential and even a necessary part of life? We argue that the current understanding of P4C implies a particular way of thinking and acting (and a particular critique) that has become the horizon of what we are addressed to think and do. How has the idea of philosophizing with children developed from an educational experiment into experimental capital?

The first section will be a genealogical excursion that explains how the concept of P4C, being disconnected from traditional forms of thinking about education and teaching, has been used to refer to a kind of philosophical potential for which the child himself or herself is responsible and that can and should become an object of educational investment. The second section indicates how today this experimental idea is developed within the discourse of P4C onto a particular subject or mode of self-understanding that draws upon a kind of apparatus of self-reflection and self-mobilization. In the conclusion we will focus on the mode of self-understanding within this self-reflective apparatus and raise the question of whether it is possible to rethink P4C, not in terms of an investment in experimental ideas but in terms of testing and modifying, not one's ideas but one's life, at the risk of one's own subjectivity.

Philosophy for Children and the Development of an Educational Experiment

Lipman developed his philosophical–educational programme in response to his concern that children in traditional forms of education do not think as well as they might. He believed (Lipman & Sharp, 1978) that schooling of autonomous citizens in a democracy could be realized only by making the child's thinking the chief business of schools. P4C was proposed as an alternative for an educational system driven only by economic and bureaucratic considerations (Lipman, 2003, p. 10). The aim of P4C was to help students to become more reflective thinkers and to gain control or mastery over the organization of their thinking and learning. Only philosophy in its active form could provide the instruments that enable children to think for themselves and make their own decisions (Lipman, 1988). Lipman proposed P4C as a potential productive investment in society. 'If children are not given the opportunity to weigh and discuss both ends and means, and their interrelationship, they are likely to become cynical about everything except their own well-being, and adults will not be slow to condemn them as "mindless little relativists"' (Lipman, 1988, p. 14). Philosophy for Lipman is not an investment in the Ideal Platonic State (Lipman, 1988, p. 15) and could not be submitted to imperatives of a social, political, cultural or religious nature.

Accordingly, Lipman's P4C programme is not based on universally generalizable principles to be known *a priori*. He turns not to Kant, but to pragmatism (Engelhart, 1997). He argues that reasonableness is not pure rationality: 'It is rationality tempered by judgment' (Lipman, 2003, p. 10). Hence, reasonableness, here, does not refer to a use of reason in which reason has no other end but itself; it refers to a use of reason in which it enables a person to explore problematic situations in everyday life in order to reach an equitable solution. Lipman writes that something is reasonable when it offers 'at least a glimpse of the direction in which we are to go' (Lipman, 2003, p. 6), or when it has proven to be useful to persuade, predominantly for logical reasons and for the quality of living together. We find the roots of Lipman's vision in the pragmatism of Dewey. Thinking for oneself can only be improved when reflecting about the consequences the individual ascertains by his actions. For Lipman, reason refers to the possibility to acquire knowledge about possible actions and reactions. This does not imply that success is guaranteed. Because we do not have at our disposal something that offers us more certainty than reflective action, we have to focus to increase the reflective quality of our actions and knowledge. It is about 'suggesting possible lines of consequence or divergence' and 'moving the discussion to a higher level of generality' (Lipman & Sharp, 1978, p. 105). Whereas Dewey connects this effort to previous experiences and additional hypotheses and observations, Lipman makes use of (in)formal logic (Daniel, 1992).

For Lipman it is not merely about mapping knowledge of diverse possibilities that can take place, but the search for knowledge of possible incorrect presuppositions in the activity of thinking about possible solutions to a problem. 'The absence of logical skills in the usual thinking skill approach ensures that little will be done to overcome students' incoherence in the formulation of explanations and arguments, in the ferreting out of underlying assumptions and implications, or in the unification of meanings' (Lipman, 1988, p. 41). Lipman writes that 'to know the causes of ideas—the conditions under which they are thought—is to liberate ourselves from intellectual rigidity and to bestow upon ourselves that power of choosing among and acting upon alternatives that is the source of intellectual freedom' (Lipman, 2003, p. 35). Critical thinking, then, means being able to make a distinction between better and weaker ways of reasoning in addition to which better ways are defined under the category of analytical thinking. In other words, according to this approach a critical thinker is someone who has at his or her disposal analytical thinking skills to acquire knowledge about underlying presuppositions: it is someone who in his or her thoughts and actions is guided by knowledge and logical principles as a source to make analyses and speculations. Consequently, for Lipman the use of analytical thinking enables one to predict what will occur and to understand the larger picture that will permit more objective judgements to account for what does occur. It means that 'each belief must be subjected to the tests of logic and experience. It does not matter whose opinions they are, or whose ideas they are—they must submit to the requirement that they be internally consistent, and their proponents must divulge the evidence that supports them' (Lipman, Sharp, & Oscanyan, 1980, p. 133).

An autonomous critical thinker in this interpretation is someone who has at his or her disposal analytical thinking skills, someone who knows how to discover prejudices and selfish reasons through acquired knowledge about himself or herself, the other and the world. Or it is someone who has to acquire analytical thinking skills in order to be critical and to think in an autonomous way. The achievement of analytical thinking skills is a necessary condition in order to be able to think and to become self-conscious. One has to be critical, but therefore one has to behave oneself in a particular way. Only a manner of thinking about philosophy that transcends the disciplines and thus implies analytical thinking skills can be called reasonable or self-conscious.

However, the question arises as to whether Lipman's interpretation of transcendence can actually be understood as transcendence. Since transcendence in Lipman's early interpretation could appear to allow the dominance of analytical thinking, it could easily be criticized for an idealism similar to that found in traditional philosophy. Lipman's reformulation of this in educational terms led him to define the role of the teacher and the community of inquiry. What is necessary, says Lipman, are professional facilitating teachers who are capable of using philosophy as a 'learning method' and thereby transform the classroom into a community of inquiry. This is a method in which contexts are created, where critical thinking is interpreted as a natural process capable of being developed, and not as something children have to appropriate (Lipman, 1980, p. 15). What constitutes P4C is a process that is experienced as a task one has to go through in order to develop critical thinking and to participate collectively. The practice of P4C cannot be simply considered as a natural process. Still, it cannot be seen as a task that is obliged since it is a practice that requires not obedience, but development. The use of P4C is related to the appeal not to be obedient to dogmatism. This appeal is the condition for being critical, implying the development of particular thinking skills and knowledge. Critical thinking in this educational–philosophical approach is thus linked to particular conditions necessary to experience oneself as someone who thinks for oneself and feels free, and these conditions refer to particular knowledge and skills.

An Educational Experiment Becomes 'Experimental' Capital

A second generation of P4C has refined many of Lipman's ideas and added new elements (Reed & Johnson, 1999). I argue now that critical rationality needs to be viewed in the complex context of multiple intersubjectivities, a so-called 'masculinist' view of rationality in its connection with the making of meaning and children's embodied experiences and emotions to show how philosophy could be redefined as the practice of an ethical subject continuously analyzing the presuppositions on which apparently transparent practices (read 'subjectivities') rest.

With the new generation, Lipman's strong emphasis on analytical thinking as a guarantee for autonomy is put under pressure. New ideas shape form: more and more notions such as plurality and intersubjectivity are being emphasized instead of logic to think about autonomy. From the 1980s onwards, P4C has been described as masculinist in its presumption of the norm.

> Equality is not the answer either since it is grounded on an essentialism that implies necessarily assimilation to a pre-existing, for the most part, male norm. Any 'essential' quality shared by all is so abstract that it excludes and/or dismisses differences among people. Moreover, the very appearance of universality depends on its congruence with the dominant sites of power. (Sheerin, 1998, p. 62)

Lipman's presumptions of a 'male' logic and analytical thinking are related to his presumption of an adult rationality into which children should grow. Walter Kohan, for example, opposes the idea of giving children access to the world of adults. 'This approach tends to legitimate the actual dominant form of rationality, and to close off space for any eventual alternative world. [...]. What might children expect from this "generous" inclusion in adult's rationality? A silencing of their voices as children?' (Kohan, 1999, p. 5). It is not so much about providing proof that children can think like adults, but that they think and that in the dominant theories of knowledge this thinking does not get the attention it deserves.

> The first step should be to recognize that [...] 'the hegemonic theory of knowledge of the day' or the 'rationalistic ideal of reason' systematically excludes children's thought and experience. Only after the deconstruction of that dominant theory of knowledge, it will be possible to reintegrate those elements of the child's episteme that have been silenced by adult rationality. (Kohan, 1999, p. 4)

Accordingly, within current discourse on P4C it is argued that neither age nor 'scholastic' development should determine someone's position as a critical thinker. Rather than thinking of the child in terms of preconceived and stable developmental structures, the child is conceived as a subject who has an individual opinion which he or she can (and has to) discover on the basis of a philosophical inquiry. This inquiry is no longer focused on the discovery of a general judgement. It becomes a method that helps the child to find out what his or her real opinions, desires and capacities are. In other words, through the community of inquiry, the child is asked to respond not to socially constituted desires but to individual drives, drives that are influenced by the permanently changing society. Hence, far more than an endless search for reasonable judgement, what is suggested in the actual discourses on P4C is that one has to find ways of encouraging self-consciousness and self-correction in children. As such, P4C is conceived of as 'a very empowering process because it brings the youngster to a point where choice is possible instead of habitual behaviour' (Kohan, 1999, p. 5).

Rondhuis and Van der Leeuw (2000, p. 33) similarly write that '[P]hilosophy is more than analysing or speculating, it has to do with the conduct of life itself, and so presupposes a readiness to reflect on and clarify experience'. Accordingly, it is argued that analytical thinking needs to be complemented with creative thinking and caring thinking (Lipman, 2003). For the child who is philosophizing, critical thinking then is no longer about getting access to 'scholastic' skills such as logical thinking but about becoming conscious of one's life process, emotions and abilities and relating oneself in an active, conductive manner towards this process. P4C increasingly appears as an investment in individual (and collective) human life: a programme that strengthens the capacity to govern one's life in a permanently changing (knowledge-based) society (Cleghorn, 2003).

In this form of subjectivity, a training in logical thinking or the acquisition of general knowledge is no longer at stake, but is replaced by a development of particular knowledge, skills and an attitude that contribute to one's personal development

(UNESCO, 2006, p. 200). In this sense, one no longer speaks about P4C in terms of a method, either. Increasingly, the practice of P4C is envisaged in terms of creating challenging environments. These environments then do not refer to a material or physical space but to symbolic spaces, contexts or zones where different meanings are circulating, where individual thinking is put under critique, where one meets other perspectives and where one can continually give renewed meaning to one's life in a safe place (UNESCO, 2006). In other words, P4C provides particular strategies, procedures and instruments which enable the individual to direct himself or herself to prior perspectives, preferences, desires and abilities. Its usefulness consists increasingly in its ability to examine the limits of one's individual perspectives, assumptions, capacities and thoughts in order to gain access to the limits of one's particular needs and problems and to become a more effective 'autonomous chooser' (Marshall, 1995; Simons and Masschelein, 2008). Being critical then, in this constellation, means the exchange of personal and well-examined perspectives and world views and the diagnosis of shortcomings that prevent the realization of this aim. The more one produces critique that stimulates the continuous making and remaking of individual and social meaning, the more one is able to transform oneself into a subject that is occupied by the development and government of one's true self. Christine Gehrett writes in this context, 'to live in a community is to increase our possibilities of accomplishing more' (1999, p. 23). To understand the community of inquiry as an environment which offers continual access to different opinions and perspectives in order to maximize the mind makes it more than a instrumental pedagogy. Autonomy, critical thinking, self-reflection and liberation are concepts that are not simply brought to light in order to react against the existing, social order and power, but have become a part of an order that experiences critical thinking as an absolute necessity to survive (Lyotard, 1999; Simons & Masschelein, 2008a).

As such, bio-power—that is, the form of power aimed at not only controlling the population but also producing and reproducing all forms of social life—is no longer an adequate term to indicate the form of power that is constituted through the discourse on P4C (Stiegler, 2010). Since a critically reflective environment offers guidelines on how to invest in life rather than giving authoritative prescriptions for how to live one's life, it becomes necessary that one keeps reflecting upon individual and collective desires and capacities. This means that within P4C one continuously experiences the need to adjust and readjust individual perspectives, thoughts or self-image, facilitated by the expertise of the professional philosopher. These are psycho-technologies stripped of the formidable theoretical framework found in other school disciplines. The teacher provides only dialogical skills, strategies and procedures that are based on philosophical knowledge that leads the individual step by step towards the production of critical potential and information to improve the quality of personal life (Simons, 2006). It is about knowledge of philosophical concepts, interpretations, analyses, questions and styles necessary to install challenging environments in order to produce the philosophical thinker, i.e. someone who has liberated himself or herself from unproductive ways of thinking.

Accordingly, the question has become 'how' to give form to one's personal development in a changing environment. Personality is no longer considered as given, characterized with inescapable temporalities and natural heaviness. It becomes something that can be modified at will, sculpted and reshaped by qualified philosophical thinkers. It becomes a matter of choice and a personal assembly of a particular array of elements on offer in a shopping mall of 'real' philosophical spirituality (Rose, 1999). Analogously, as Rose (1999, p. 271–272) suggests, thinking for oneself ceases to be the external expression of an inner truth or a movement towards universal standardized categories and becomes a matter of acquired competences, knowledge and skills of self-government and self-awareness.

Although critical thinking continues to exist, the process is all encompassing. In sum, before individuals can act and think for themselves and before they can act critically on the basis of their own thoughts, they 'must first become the kind of person interested in and capable of relating to themselves as their responsible agents of their own conduct' (Masschelein, 2004, p. 361).

P4C, Ethos and Experimental Education

In what follows I want to explore another idea of philosophy for children,[1] which works upon power relations. I want to articulate an idea of philosophy with children in which philosophy will be conceived of not as the practice of a legislating subject passing judgement on a deficient reality, but as the practice of an ethical subject analysing the presuppositions on which apparently transparent practices (read 'subjectivities') rest. Here, the adversary of philosophy with children is not the formation of a subject, but its disclosure or perhaps undoing the closure of the subject. This does not mean the same as 'deconstruction', if this word supposes an edifice composed of demonstration and analysis.

I have tried to show that what makes P4C so important to a thriving society is a permanent reactivation of a critical attitude that is called into being by and through programmes such as P4C. While P4C explicitly criticizes traditional education for its focus on the generalizable principles and knowledge to be known in order to become an autonomous subject, it does not free the subject from this idea. Using Foucault's reformulation of Kant's conception of 'Aufklärung', it can be argued that while Lipman's philosophical programme no longer depends on a fundamental universalism about humankind, its 'intellectual blackmail' (Foucault, 1984, p. 6) remains. After all, it is from the pursuit of humanism that the idea of thinking for oneself derives its dynamics. Even where it precludes a universal idea of human being, it seems that it remains bound to a particular rationality (or subjectivity) that can be read as the limits within which thinking, acting and hoping have to stay in order to reach true knowledge, right action and worthwhile desire.

Inspired by Foucault, in what follows I will try to articulate another idea of what philosophy for children could be about. These inquiries may be viewed not from the perspective of a search for formal structures with universal value, but rather as a genealogical investigation into the events that have led us to constitute ourselves and to recognize ourselves as subjects of what we are doing, thinking and saying (Foucault, 1984, p. 6). At that point, these kinds of inquiry are characterized by a limit-attitude or a work done at the limits of that what makes up our reality and that constitutes ourselves and our way of doing, thinking and saying in that reality. What is at stake here is explicitly a *limit-attitude* or an *ethos* constituting the search for the limits of what can be thought, felt and said in a particular time and space. Critique then means an analysis and reflection upon these limits: on these features that constitute ourselves as critical beings, for instance. Now, it could be said that this is also what is at stake in P4C. However, whereas for Lipman critique is about legitimating what the limits of knowledge are, a philosophical inquiry that is characterized by a limit-attitude starts from the question: To what extent is what is given to us as universal, necessary and obligatory, singular or the product of an arbitrary act? This comes down to a transformation of critique conducted in the form of a necessary limitation into a practical critique that takes the form of a limit-experience (Foucault, 1984, p. 6). An obvious implication of this transformation is that the practice of critique no longer functions as a search for (in)formal structures that are dominating or oppressive but becomes a search for structures or power relations that have a conductive force (Foucault, 1984). This means that critique is about a detailed analysis of the ways of thinking, acting, wanting and feeling that have made up our present, and that have constituted us in that present as a subject. As a result, this kind of critical analysis always is an analysis of what we want ourselves. After all, critique is not unrelated to what we want but activated only through our will and purpose (Simons & Masschelein, 2008b, p. 15).

This is not an attempt to write about ourselves in terms of identity. Instead, it is a concern to develop an analysis that makes visible 'the vectors that shape our relation to ourselves moving from the question "what kind of selves have we become?" to "how do we relate to ourselves as selves of a certain kind"' (Rabinow & Rose, 2003). In that sense, critique here is that practice in which one is concerned with 'truth through which we constitute ourselves as subjects acting on others' and with 'ethics through which we constitute ourselves as moral agents' (Hacking, 2002, p. 2). In thinking of constituting ourselves as moral agents, as Hacking writes, we think of constituting ourselves as so and so. Yet we are concerned, in the end, with possible ways to be a person (Hacking, 2002). And this concern has an ethical component as well. Ethical, here, however, does not refer to the constitution of moral agents as something that is generalizable for all rational beings and that forms the universal structure of all thinking and of all action. On the contrary, we constitute ourselves at a place and time, using materials that have a distinctive and historically formed organization. 'The ethical component to be unravelled then is how we, as people in civilisations with histories, have become moral agents, through constituting ourselves as moral agents in specific, local historical ways' (Hacking, 2002, p. 2). Critical thought adopts a particular relation to ethics, in the sense that it allows one to step back from a particular way of acting and thinking: to present it to oneself as an object of thought in terms of its meaning, its conditions and its goals. Critical thinking is the movement by which one detaches oneself from one's mode of thinking and acting, establishing it as an object, and reflecting on it as a problem. This kind of thinking is not autonomous in any of the strong senses given in Western philosophy. Critical thinking, as it is understood here, is neither transparent nor a passive waiting or an intentional act of consciousness. It is not necessarily coherent, it has no univocal or foundational meaning that is amenable to a completely reasonable clarification. It is not an external evaluation of a situation. Critical thinking, here, is the transformation of what is given as universal, necessary and obligatory into a question that needs a response. This kind of thinking then can be considered as ethical, in the sense that it separates us out from the contingency that has made us who we are, and what we do or think. This separation does not lead us to a search for the truth that in the end becomes a science (knowledge). It is a separation that gives 'new impetus, as far and wide as possible, to the undefined work of freedom' (Foucault, 1984, p. 6). This means that the thinker is neither entirely outside the situation in question nor entirely enmeshed within it. It means that the thinker is present in the present, exposed to what is happening here and now: no longer in the position to stay where one is because confronted with the question of how to live the present.

To put it briefly, from the idea of a limit-attitude the critical thinker goes looking for different attitudes towards the present. Accordingly, this limit-attitude is always an experimental attitude (Simons & Masschelein, 2008b). It is the thinker that experiments with the self. More precisely, he or she experiments with the way he or she lives in the present (Simons & Masschelein, 2008b). From the idea of a limit-attitude the personal thoughts, feelings and actions of the critical thinker are also at stake, by which a space opens to look differently to the self, others and the world, and to stay no longer who one is or is supposed to be. Lipman has acknowledged the importance of the making of meaning, but this aspect tends to have been overlooked by those who focus on his analytical methods. Teaching philosophy becomes an issue of attitude, an attitude that has something to do with an openness for the child who continually engages with the process of constructing self. The child here is not the same as the not-yet-reasonable or autonomous subject. It refers rather to the completely other than the self, so that it may arrive as the potentiality to question and decompose the process of subjectivation, and therefore exercises in syllogistic logic or metaphor serve only as means to the end of forming reasons as a basis for autonomous choice to become.

Concluding Thoughts

Philosophy for Children has been shown to have the potentiality to 'desubjectify'. This potentiality encloses both the essence of education and its critique. Philosophy is not synonymous with education. We want to suppose that philosophy is what makes education possible. The ambition of education is to bring order, while philosophy disorders. P4C tries to combine both terms, which, at first sight, seems to be an impossibility. Education is envisaged as a method that has to bring the child to a particular destiny and determination, but this way of thinking about childhood and education prevents the child from being critical. We have argued that the figure of the autonomous chooser in education is related to a particular subject(ivity) which can be described and defined in terms of yet fixated capacities or needs to be realized or articulated: education uses a way of thinking that embeds the child, rather than lifting it out of its bed. We propose a radical rethinking of the child, not in terms of developmental characteristics, but in a way that makes the child the agent of himself or herself, through a desubjectifying or limit-experience, a way of thinking that experiences childhood (the child) as a question, irreducible, never relative towards something else in terms of causal relation or judgement.

This way of thinking about philosophy for children has a double task: exploring a kind of thinking that starts from the irreducible, and asking oneself the question of how to live with it. Therefore, thinking about one's life using the structures that constitute our thoughts, actions and feelings can no longer form the focal point of education. What philosophy for children enlightens is our possibility to think. It provokes the experience that we are (still) not thinking, even if thinking forms the focal point of education. This consciousness, however, is not science; it is an opening. It is experiencing a desire to think, confronted with the unthinkable and the unbearable ... with something all too human to think. This desire refers to the indescribable need to go and to see without knowing what there is to see. Hence, philosophy for children in this self-understanding does not seek to discover knowledge about the self, the other or the world. It directs oneself to live *with* the unpredictability of the self, the other and the world. It directs oneself to the rhythm of life, let's say, to what comes.

Acknowledgements

I am grateful to Felicity Haynes for her corrections to an earlier version of this paper.

Note

1. Here 'philosophy for children', without capitals, refers no longer to a particular movement or content, but to the possibility to rethink it.

References

Cleghorn, P. (2002). Why philosophy with children? *Education Review, 15*, 47–51.

Daniel, M. F. (1992). *La Philosophie et les enfants. L'enfant philosophe. Le programme de Lipman et l'influence de Dewey.* (Montréal: Les éditions Logiques).

Engelhart, S. (1997). *Modelle und Perspektiven der Kinderphilosophie.* Heinsberg: Agentur Dieck.

Foucault, M. (1984). What is Enlightening? (Qu'est-ce que les Lumières?). In P. Rabinow & N. Rose (Eds.), *The Foucault reader* (pp. 32–50). New York: Pantheon Books. Retrieved August 5, 2010, from http://anthropos-lab.net/wp/publications/2009/04/Rabinow-Rose-Intro-Essential.pdf

Gehrett, C. (1999). Children as revolutionaries: Transforming the paradigms. In H. Palsson, B. Siguroardottir & B.B. Nelson (Eds.), *Philosophy for children on top of the world. Proceedings of the Eighth International Conference on Philosophy with Children* (pp. 48–65). Iceland: University of Akureyri.

Hacking, I. (2002). *Historical ontology.* Cambridge, MA: Harvard University Press.

Kohan, W. (1999). What can philosophy and children offer each other? *Journal of Philosophy for Children, 14*, 2–8.

Lipman, M. (1988). *Philosophy goes to school.* Philadelphia, PA: Temple University Press.

Lipman, M. (2003). *Thinking in education.* Cambridge: Cambridge University Press.

Lipman, M., & Sharp, A. M. (1978). *Growing up with philosophy.* Philadelphia, PA: Temple University Press.

Lipman, M., Sharp, A., & Oscanyan, F. S. (1980). *Philosophy in the classroom.* Philadelphia, PA: Temple University Press.

Lyotard, J. F. (1999). *The post modern condition: A report on knowledge*. Minneapolis, MN: University of Minnesota Press.

Marshall, J. D. (1995). Foucault and neo-liberalism: Bio-power and busno-power. In A. Neiman (Ed.), *Proceedings of the Philosophy of Education Society*. Illinois: Philosophy of Education Society.

Masschelein, J. (2004). How to conceive of critical educational theory today? *Journal of Philosophy of Education, 38*, 351–367.

Rabinow, P., & Rose, N. (2003). Foucault today. In P. Rabinow & N. Rose (Eds.), *The essential Foucault: Selections from the essential works of Foucault* (pp. 1954–1984). New York: New Press.

Reed, R. F., & Johnson, T. W. (1999). *Friendship and moral education. Twin pillars of philosophy for children*. New York: Peter Lang.

Rondhuis, T., & Van der Leeuw, K. (2000). Performance and progress in philosophy. An attempt at operationalisation of criteria. *Teaching Philosophy, 23*, 23–42.

Rose, N. (1999). *Governing the soul. The shaping of the private self*. London: Free Association Books).

Sheerin, M. T. (1998). Processes of justice in community. *Analytic Teaching, 18*, 61–64.

Simons, M. (2006). Learning as investment: Notes on governmentality and biopolitics. *Educational Philosophy and Theory, 38*(4), 523–540.

Simons, M., & Masschelein, J. (2008a). From schools to learning environments: the dark side of being exceptional. *Journal of Philosophy of Education, 42*(3), 687–704.

Simons, M. & Masschelein, J. (2008b). Over Kritisch e-ducatieve studies. In J. Masschelein & M. Simons (Eds.). *De schaduwzijde van onze welwillendheid. Kritische Studies van de pedagogische actualiteit*. (pp. 7–24). Leuven: Acco.

Stiegler, B. (2010). *Taking care of youth and the generations*, trans. S. Barker. California: Stanford University Press.

UNESCO. (2007). *Philosophy. A school of freedom*. Paris: UNESCO Publishing.

Vansieleghem, N. (2007). Public space in a network society? A note on the call for public space (Philosophy) in education today. In P. Smeyers & M. Depaepe (Eds.), *Educational research: Networks and technologies* (pp. 137–148). Dordrecht: Springer.

Index